Table of Contents

This comprehensive review of public library policy could not be more timely. Two of the key priorities among the Government's overall policy objectives are:

- to ensure that Ireland moves rapidly to embrace the opportunities of the Information Society so as to support economic and social progress as well as a more participative democracy; and

- to establish an inclusive society in which all citizens can participate fully in the social and economic life of the country.

Our report demonstrates that the public library system has the potential to make a major contribution to furthering both of these important objectives. It is a service that is already widely-used, is widely-appreciated but whose merits are somewhat taken for granted. Library infrastructure, although not complete, has over 1000 service points throughout the country. Also, the training and expertise of library staff is particularly suited to the responsibility of guiding citizens of all backgrounds through the learning, enlightenment and public information opportunities that are now available.

In our report, we identify what is necessary to enable this potential to be achieved, both in terms of completing the infrastructure and in terms of a range of measures to improve the availability, accessibility and quality of the services provided.

In relation to infrastructure, we pay particular attention to the necessary investment in information and communications technology in public libraries, which will complement the Government's current programme of similar investment in our schools.

From our own discussions on the project team, from our consultations with interested parties and from the submissions which we have received, we see a clear recognition on the part of library professionals, local authority members and officials in local and central government that there is now an opportunity to position the public library service to make a very substantial contribution to economic and social progress for all our people. We also see an enthusiasm on all sides to respond flexibly and constructively to ensure that the opportunity is taken.

I am pleased to commend the report to the Minister for the Environment and Local Government and to all those whose responses to its recommendations will determine what contribution the public library system ultimately makes to the achievement of a more inclusive society which can fully exploit the benefits of the Information Age.

Tom O'Mahony
October 1998

two

Description of
Methodology & Scope

2

2.1 Background

This report has been prepared by a project team specially established by the Minister for the Environment and Local Government to review public library policy in Ireland.

The Terms of Reference for the project are:

The Project Team will submit to the Minister for the Environment and Local Government, a report on Public Libraries in Ireland within twelve months of its establishment.

The report will address the following issues:

- The current position of public libraries

- The evolving role of public libraries in the areas of information provision and cultural/heritage services

- The roles played by the Department of the Environment and Local Government, An Chomhairle Leabharlanna and Local Authorities in the development of public library services.

- Financial arrangements for library infrastructure and services.

- Recommendations to the Minister for the development of the public library service.

The Project Team shall co-operate with other projects engaged in similar research.

The Project Team shall consult where necessary with interested parties.

The Project Team consists of representatives from the bodies most concerned with managing and delivering the public library service in Ireland. The team comprises:

Mr. Tom O'Mahony (Chairman),
Mr. Tim Mawe,
- *representing the Department of the Environment and Local Government;*

Mr. Liam Ronayne, Donegal County Librarian,
Ms. Deirdre Ellis-King, Dublin City Librarian,
- *representing the Library Association of Ireland;*

Norma McDermott, Director,
- *representing An Chomhairle Leabharlanna;*

Mr. Eddie Breen, Waterford City Manager,
Mr. Brian Johnston, Cavan County Manager,
- *representing the City and County Managers Association;*

Cllr. Frank Prendergast, Limerick
Cllr. Ita Fox, Sligo,
- *representing the General Council of County Councils;*

Cllr. Michael Joy, Tramore, Co. Waterford,
- *representing the Association of Municipal Authorities of Ireland*

The Secretary to the Project Team is Ms. Veronica Healy, Department of the Environment and Local Government.

The Project Team held its first meeting on 10 September 1997 and met a further 10 times. The final meeting of the project team was held on 8 October 1998, when this report was agreed.

2.2 Scope

The scope of the review and the methodology used to carry it out was agreed by the project team following discussions on where the library service is today, the context in which it operates and the impetus that exists for change.

The project team agreed to structure the review as follows:

Prepare a comprehensive analysis of the existing library service which looks at:
- Objectives and priorities of the public library service
- Range and quality of services provided
- Accessibility to the service (including opening

hours, social barriers, charges, physical access for disabled)

- Accessibility to library material (including loan periods, overdues, inter-library loans)
- Marketing of library services
- Staffing (including numbers, grading, training and development)
- Infrastructure (including buildings, mobiles, ICT other equipment and stock)
- Organisation (including roles played by Department of the Environment and Local Government, An Chomhairle Leabharlanna, Library Authorities, Institutions of the EU and other international organisations, Public Representatives, Users and Non-users)
- Funding (including the distribution of capital allocations to the library service by the Department of the Environment and Local Government and funding allocated to the library service by local authorities)
- A synthesis of Library Development Programmes prepared under the Local Government Act 1994.

Prepare an analysis which compares the existing situation with relevant other countries and other sectors.

Describe the needs that a public library service should meet. This will include:

- Public Information
- Cultural and Heritage Resource
- Educational Resource
- Community Resource/Public Space
- Local Authority Interface

This analysis will also include a projection as to how the needs described are likely to change over the next 5-10 years.

Prepare a description of what the library service should be like in 5 years time. This will be a high level description that outlines the services that should be available, the standards that should be attained in terms of infrastructure and how they should be organised.

Set out the measures required by all the players to enable the needs for the library service to be realised. These measures may be of a financial, organisational or legislative nature. They must be feasible. The scale and scope of the measures will take into account the level of funding that is potentially available for library developments in coming years. A subset of the measures required will be addressed to the Minister for the Environment and Local Government as recommendations. They will be specific, costed, affordable and programmed.[i]

2.3 Methodology

The Project Team operated within this scope and made some adjustments to its approach as the review progressed. The work of the project team has been carried out in five stages. These were as follows:

Stage 1: Project initiation
A Project Outline and Discussion Paper was presented to the project team for discussion. These documents set out the methodology and the scope of the project respectively.

Stage 2: Research
The project team sought submissions from interested parties in relation to public libraries and consulted with a number of key players in delivering the public library service.

The project team considered research carried out in the field of public libraries, both in Ireland and in other countries. It also considered other initiatives that impact on public libraries, such as Ireland's response to the Information Society and the Strategic Management Initiative within local authorities.

Two members of the project team also participated in the Working Group which oversees the preparation of the National Policy for Libraries and Information Studies. The Chairman of the project team is also Chairman of the Consultative Council of that project.

Stage 3: Policy options

The project team examined and discussed the policy options flowing from Stage 2 and have agreed a set of proposals that are specific, costed, relevant, desirable and achievable.

Stage 4: Report

The project team has prepared this report. It contains:

- a vision of the public library service.

- an analysis of the public library service, including a review of the roles played by the Department of the Environment and Local Government, An Chomhairle Leabharlanna and Local Authorities in the development of the service;

- a summary of the views expressed to the project team on the development of the public library service;

- an account of the policy issues involved and the project team's views on those issues;

- recommendations to the Minister for the Environment and Local Government for the development of the public library service. The report also contains recommendations addressed to other key players in delivering the public library service, notably library authorities, An Chomhairle Leabharlanna, the Minister for Education and Science and the Minister for Arts, Heritage, Gaeltacht and the Islands.

Stage 5: Post-report

The project team now submits this report to the Minister for consideration by him and by other Ministers. The project team understands that the report will be published by the Department of the Environment and Local Government.

The project team makes some proposals in Chapter 8 of this report concerning the implementation of the recommendations made by the project team.

Notes

i   Internal Scoping Document agreed by the project team

three

Report Summary

3

The subsequent chapters of this report deal in a comprehensive way with the issues facing public libraries in Ireland today and outline a strategy for their development.

Chapter 4 sets out a **vision of a public library service** that is designed to meet the needs of Irish people into the next millennium. It defines the role of the public library in the Information Age and positions the Irish public library service within broader public policy. In this chapter, the project team also reviews the social impact of the library service and describes a future for the service that is built upon a premise that public libraries should be judged, not on what they are but on what they do.

The future library service is described as one which:

- will provide open and democratic access to the world of information;
- will be a locally-based support for life-long learning;
- will continue to provide access to the sum of human thought and imagination in a self-directed fashion, and
- will be a community-based support to literacy-training and reading, particularly for young people.

Chapter 5 gives an **overview of public libraries to-day**. It contains summary information on the range of services provided and on the level of infrastructure, usage and service delivery. It also describes the structures in place for delivering the service. This chapter also makes an assessment of the current position in relation to:

- library usage
- range and quality of stock
- marketing of library services
- staffing of libraries
- information and communication technologies infrastructure
- charges for library services

Chapter 6 synthesises the **views expressed** to the project team by members of the public and by interested organisations. Almost 800 submissions were received. Some of the key submissions are sum-marised in the chapter and the views of all submissions are analysed.

The key issues raised are:

the need to deliver a better library service to meet changes in Irish society by:

- developing enhanced opening hours;
- investing in library staff;
- improving equality of access to library services;
- improving specialised services;
- improving libraries information services;
- developing life-long learning services;

the need to provide adequate infrastructure - a network of modern, properly equipped and staffed service points covering the entire country that will ensure libraries play a key role in the information society;

the need to develop new service-delivery methods that will enable areas of low population and other isolated communities to have equal access to library services in a cost-efficient manner;

the need to improve the range and quality of stock;.

the need to improve local and national marketing of library services;

the need to improve co-operation between libraries and with other organisations;

the need to improve schools library services;

the need to develop the library as a centre of culture;

the need to improve the service through library research.

These issues are discussed in more detail in **Chapter 7**. This chapter also includes a range of recommendations addressed to the Minister for the Environment and Local Government, to other Ministers, to An Chomhairle Leabharlanna and to library authorities.

The recommendations can be categorised as **Strategic**, **Financial** and **Service-delivery**.

The **strategic** recommendations include:

The project team recommends to the Minister that the public library infrastructure and services be developed to form a key component of a society that appreciates and understands the value of information, knowledge and learning. The library service should, therefore, be an important participant in government initiatives to develop what is known as an Information Society.

The project team recommends to the Minister that the investment in library infrastructure and services should enhance equity of access to information and that it should form part of the Government's National Anti-Poverty Strategy.

The project team recommends to the Minister that there should be a national commitment to information access through public libraries. This should link to issues relating to information technology access, public information and freedom of information. It might take the form of a charter whereby the State guarantees that every citizen should be able to access all information at, or through, the local public library.

The project team recommends to the Government that the public library service should be put at the heart of public delivery initiatives of electronic government.

If Ireland is to move successfully towards electronic government that is equally accessible to all, it is essential that the necessary infrastructure is put in place through the public library system.

In order to promote equality of access to the public library service, the project team recommends that each library authority should develop and implement a strategy to improve access to the library for everybody. The strategy should seek to overcome physical barriers to library use, social barriers to library use and financial barriers to library use.

The project team recommends that An Chomhairle Leabharlanna should work closely with the Information Society Commission to ensure that the public library service is an integral part of measures to develop awareness of the information society.

The project team recommends that the Department of Environment and Local Government and An Chomhairle Leabharlanna should have a formal relationship with the Department of Education and Science centred on arrangements for life-long learning.

The project team recommends that An Chomhairle Leabharlanna accepts the role of marketing public libraries at national level. The project team clearly sees this role as being different to running national advertising campaigns or other promotional activities. It should focus on the contribution that the library can make to issues such as ICT awareness, literacy and lifelong learning.

The project team recommends to library authorities that they develop a library co-operation strategy. The strategy will develop an approach to resource sharing and better service provision that will embrace co-operation with other libraries and also with a wide range of groups and organisations operating locally.

The project team recommends that library authorities move rapidly towards implementing a network for resource-sharing. As a first step, a nation-wide sharing of catalogue data, using the measures recommended for ICT development, should be put in place.

The project team recommends that a national focus should be placed on co-operation. Accordingly, the 32 strategies for each library authority area should be incorporated into a national strategy which can be used to agree appropriate measures with all players at national and international level.

The project team recommends that the remit, composition and services of EuroFocus on Libraries be expanded to embrace all levels and sectors of international library co-operation. EuroFocus should be seen as a pro-active element in an overall advisory service provided to library authorities.

The project team recommends that a local strategy for developing co-operation with other educational services should be incorporated into the library co-operation strategy. An Chomhairle Leabharlanna, in association with the Department of Education and Science, should support and assist this process.

In order to accelerate the development of schools libraries, the project team recommends to the Minister that he facilitate a dialogue between library authorities, An Chomhairle Leabharlanna, the Department of Environment and Local Government and the Department of Education and Science. This dialogue would consider how best schools libraries might develop and would take account of the issues arising for all parties. This dialogue would also address the development of post-primary school library services.

With the expansion and diversification of arts provision, both locally and nationally, the project team recommends that a national strategy on delivering of the arts, in a way that is more accessible to the wider community than has been available heretofore, should be established. Such a strategy should take as its starting point the report of the Public Libraries and the Arts project.

The project team recommends that the Arts Council, in formulating and in implementing the next Arts Plan, should take account of the positive role that libraries can play in developing the full spectrum of the arts in Ireland. This is particularly important for communities that do not have access to any other arts infrastructure.

The project team also recommends that An Chomhairle Leabharlanna should co-ordinate a submission to the Department of Arts, Heritage, Gaeltacht and the Islands concerning the preparation of the National Heritage Plan. The project team also recommends that library authorities participate fully in the preparation of the National Heritage Plan.

In order to improve the research climate and by implication to improve the quality of library services, the project team recommends that a co-ordinated approach to Irish public library research should be undertaken. This should be formalised as a Public Libraries Research Programme, with specific terms of reference and an identifiable budget.

The **Financial** recommendations include

The project team recommends to the Minister that a revised programme for investment in library infrastructure and services be put in place. The revised programme would address all the issues necessary to provide a comprehensive library service.

The project team recommends to the Minister that at least £55 million should be provided directly by the Exchequer, in the period 1999 to 2006, for a revised programme of investment in library infrastructure. This comprises just under 60% of the funding necessary to provide a level of infrastructure, including ICT infrastructure, which will allow equitable access to library services.

The project team recommends to the Minister that a cap on funding of individual projects should be set at 75% of the agreed cost of the project.

The project team recommends that the balance of funding should be provided by library authorities and where appropriate should be raised from other sources such as corporate sponsorship.

The project team recommends that the Minister for Finance should provide tax-relief in respect of donations made to library authorities from individuals and organisations in respect of library development. The relief should be in line with that available for gifts for education in the arts.

The project team recommends to the Minister, that a national approach be taken to ICT provision. The ICT provision will be aimed at making 'content' available to everybody by:

- giving access to the human record in whatever form it might be stored, in electronic formats as well as printed materials and multi-media;
- giving access to all government services, local and national;
- giving nation-wide access to all public library catalogues;
- making local business and community information accessible on-line;
- using ICT to offer full text, images, sound etc.;
- providing electronic document delivery;
- providing access to networks and support for net-navigation and info-searching;
- providing workstations for the public to create their own content;
- providing open learning and training opportunities;
- creating interfaces between the internet and on-line catalogues;
- digitising local studies materials;

The project team recommends that up to 75% of the cost of the investment should be available from the Exchequer. The proposed investment will cover connectivity, hardware (new or upgraded), maintenance, training and up-skilling for staff and training and tutoring for the public.

The first steps to be taken are to provide Internet access to the public through all public libraries and to complete the automation of housekeeping functions of libraries.

The project team recommends to the Minister that the Department of the Environment and Local Government should co-fund the provision of optical scanners at a rate of 50% in respect of 125 scanners over 3 years.

The project team recommends to the Minister that he makes a small allocation available to pilot some innovative solutions in delivering library services to isolated communities. The sum available might be £100,000 over two years. The pilot projects might be carried out and co-funded in association with other government departments which are trying to tackle similar problems in respect of their services.

While recognising the general difficulties faced by library authorities, the project team strongly recommends that a programme of bookfund increases be undertaken by each library authority. The project team also recommends that a national target should be agreed by all library authorities. It is proposed that the target would be that by 2002, each library authority would invest at least £2.50 per capita in bookstock annually.

In order to help library authorities achieve the necessary increase, the project team recommends to the Minister he should allocate a national book grant totalling £3.6 million over four years from 1999. This should be structured as follows: 1999: £1,000,000; 2000: £1,000,000; 2001: £800,000 and 2002: £800,000.

The project team recommends to the Minister for Education and Science that the per capita increases for general bookfunds implemented by library authorities should be matched by increases in the per capita bookfund grant for primary school libraries made by the Department of Education and Science.

The project team also recommends that the Minister for Education and Science should consider providing a specific bookfund grant in respect of post-primary schools where a school library is in operation.

The project team recommends that a review of library charges should be undertaken by each library authority during 1999. This review should focus on:

- the structure of charges
- the scale of charges
- the cost of administering charges
- the level of service provided in respect of charges
- the equity of membership charges taking into account ability to pay.

The **service delivery** recommendations include:

The project team recommends that library authorities should immediately commence work on developing a programme of enhanced opening hours. These should begin to be implemented during 1999.

Library authorities should recognise the long term commitment of their staff in a concrete way and devote the investment in human resources needed to take the library service into the new century.

The project team recommends that library authorities should carry out a fundamental review of how it serves isolated communities, whether rural or urban. Library authorities should be prepared to use innovative solutions to meet identified needs.

In order to address the need to provide access to library services to people with disabilities, the project team recommends that library authorities should include in their access strategy, measures to bring all of their libraries into compliance with Part M of the Building Regulations by 2006.

The project team recommends to local authorities that they maximise the use of public

libraries in providing access by the public to all of their services, so that the library becomes a gateway to government at local level.

In order to market library services effectively, the project team recommends that each library authority carry out a programme of research into what their users and the public in their area want from the library.

The project team recommends that all library staff should have a detailed knowledge of cultural resources available. This should be developed as an integrated part of the Library Staff Development Plan.

The project team recommends that library authorities put in place a staff mobility policy aimed at extending public access to specialist knowledge throughout the library area of responsibility. This policy may include placements or staff-exchanges with other cultural institutions such as museums or archives.

The project team recommends to the Minister that he request the Minister for Arts, Heritage, Gaeltacht and the Islands to initiate a national programme on the digitisation of library collections of high cultural value.

The project team recommends that An Chomhairle Leabharlanna, in association with a selection of Library Authorities and broadcasters, should research the costs and benefits of generating a greater public library presence in the mass media, focused on providing greater access to cultural resources held in the public library.

Chapter 8 of the report proposes to the Minister, to An Chomhairle Leabharlanna and to Library Authorities the **next steps** each might take in order to implement the recommendations of this report.

four

Vision of Library Service

4

4.1 Why have a public library service?

The public library is for everybody. It is a resource for each individual and group in Ireland. It is a multi-purpose service, meeting different needs in different ways.

"Libraries do not, however, exist as an end in themselves. The project team believes that library services in Ireland should be judged, not by what they are, but by what they do."

The project team sees the public library not as a building or an institution, but as a resource to be used by people, one that is built on three pillars of equal importance:

- it is a resource for Information and Learning
- it is a resource for Culture and the Imagination
- it is a resource for Children and Young people.

Libraries do not, however, exist as an end in themselves. The project team believes that library services in Ireland should be judged, not by what they are, but by what they do.

The project team believes that there is a public need for open and democratic access to the world of information, whether in written, spoken or electronic formats.

The project team believes that there is a need for locally-based support services to life-long learning.

The project team believes that there is a need for a service which provides access to the accumulated sum of human thought and imagination.

The project team believes that there is a need for a community-based service to support literacy and reading, particularly amongst young people.

The project team believes that the public library service, properly resourced and managed can most effectively meet these needs for the Irish people.

The project team believes that the library service can equally meet the needs of all users, whether they are researching particular subjects, casually browsing through the available resources or simply using the library as a quiet place to read or study.

These are not new needs and the public library is not a new response. The public library service has a long tradition in meeting these needs. From before the provision of the Carnegie libraries early this century through to the current National Lottery-funded libraries, there has been recognition of the value of libraries in meeting society's needs. In a recent survey, 71% of the public agreed that it is well worth spending time in a public library.[ii]

However, like many other fundamental services in Ireland, the value of the library service to the community is not often explicitly stated.

Nevertheless, the Minister for the Environment and Local Government, Mr. Noel Dempsey, T.D., has already noted the value and the role of public libraries. Speaking in Co. Roscommon in February, 1998, he stated that:

"the public library and its learning power is a source of inclusion. It belongs to us all and everybody is welcome here. There is no elitism or exclusivity. Nobody needs to justify their presence in a library....."

If we are serious about developing an economy that can continue to compete with our neighbours in the twenty-first century, it is essential that we provide the tools to enable us to compete. The tools that we need are information and knowledge.

"Nobody needs to justify their presence in a library....."

And, if we are serious about developing individual citizens that feel at home in our society, it is essential that we provide the resources and the structures that allow people to develop. The resources we need include a common place where we can go and develop ourselves, either individually or as part of a group. These tools and resources are available...in the library."[iii]

This endorsement chimes well with the views of the former Minister, Mr. Brendan Howlin, T.D. Speaking in Galway, in January 1997, he noted that:

" it is important [to state the value of libraries] because we tend to take libraries for granted. In one way this is a tribute to the place that libraries have in Ireland. They are a tremendously well-established cultural network.

The library service has been assimilated into the community in a way that many other cultural services have not. Going to the library is part of everyday life for many people; whereas going to a gallery or theatre or museum is still a special occasion.

Our familiarity with libraries is partly due to their availability. They are to be found in every major town in Ireland and in many smaller ones. Libraries are part of the community and are trusted in a way that other public institutions may not be".[iv]

The appreciation of the value of libraries is not confined to Ireland or to the library sector looking at itself. The Out of Hours Report,[v] a study of town centre decline and renewal in Britain, published in 1991, found that the library was perceived to be important because:

" it was used by a wider cross-section of the local population than almost any other public, commercial or retail institution in the town centre; it was an important resource for the elderly, both for book-borrowing and newspaper-reading; it was a focal point for children and parents, and for school use; ... it was felt to be a safe environment in which to meet people, sit and browse, or use without payment or pressure (an increasingly rare use of space in the modern town centre)."

More recently, Better Local Government: A Programme for Change[vi] referred to Irish public libraries in the context of more general reforms of local government. It stated that:

> *" The role of libraries continues to evolve. The library service now acts as an information and educational resource, runs programmes of outreach and participates in partnerships with other groups."*

" The role of libraries continues to evolve. The library service now acts as an information and educational resource, runs programmes of outreach and participates in partnerships with other groups."

The public library service is also seen internationally as being a part of broader social policy. The former President of the European Commission, Mr. Jacques Delors has pointed to the crucial relationship between employment, exclusion and education in an article entitled "Social exclusion: what governments can do"[vii]. He states that the challenge facing society is to:

" strike a balance between collective and individual responsibility against a background of economic, technological and geopolitical upheavals which have turned social policy upside-down. The most obvious answer is to transform and improve our education systems...High skills and jobs mobility make the availability of training for adults indispensable"

The improvement foreseen by Delors would make life-long learning and adult education part of a seamless system which would equip everyone with four types of learning:

- learning to know: a general background provides the passport to lifelong education, giving people a taste, but also laying the foundation for learning throughout life;

- learning to do: learning to move from traditional jobs by acquiring more general skills will help people adapt to the changing workplace, reinforcing their employability;

- learning to be: the need to exercise a greater independence combined with a stronger sense of personal responsibility. None of the talents in every person should be left untapped. This is one of the most efficient weapons against exclusion;

- learning to live together: this means creating a new spirit of common understanding, fostering a desire to participate actively in society and rejecting all forms of racism."

These four aspects of learning, crucial to a system of life-long learning which in turn is necessary to maintain economic and social development, are all facilitated by the resources, services and activities of a vibrant public library service.

4.2   The public library service in broader public policy

The previous section of this reports sets out the value of public libraries. However, the project team sees the library as a component of a broader-based approach which gives everybody access to information, learning and culture as well as providing support services to people who need them.

This approach interacts with other public policies, in particular that of creating an equitable "Information Society"

It is a cornerstone of policy making for the Ireland of the twenty-first century that we must embrace the opportunities of the Information Age or be left behind economically, socially and culturally. The Information Society is much discussed but little defined. In essence, it will mean a society and an economy built on the creation, storage, and multi-faceted use of information using the most modern information and communications technologies, implying the widest possible access to that information.

The Irish government's vision for the Information Society is that:

"Ireland is a unique community, rich in culture, learning and creativity where the Information Society is embraced:

- to support the talents of our people;
- to create employment, wealth and vibrant, inclusive communities;

and where citizens participate more actively in government".[viii]

This echoes the sentiments of similar statements elsewhere; for instance the Canadian Government's view is that:

"In the new global economy, where knowledge is the key resource, the quality of the nation's human resources is critical to ensuring competitiveness. The key to prosperity in the knowledge economy is for workers to make intelligent use of information. Learning must span all our working lives."[ix]

The European Union has also embraced the social aspect of the Information Society. The European Commission's opinion on the social and labour market dimension of the Information Society was published earlier this year.[x] It emphasises that the Information Society is for all and that public policies can make the difference. It notes in Chapter II that: "Modern infrastructure, applications and services should be available at affordable prices. ...The availability of personal computers and Internet access in the home remains predominantly the preserve of those with higher incomes and educational attainment levels. This rapidly changing technological context means that universal service is a dynamic and evolving concept which must be kept under review if it is to respond to people's needs and expectations. Access to advanced services and applications through public access points such as libraries, schools and other community meeting points is regarded by some as a proxy to universal services."

"The Information Society is not just about Information and Communication Technology. It is about social change"

The Commission concludes this section by declaring as its **objective**: "Ensure access for all by promoting availability, affordability, accessibility and awareness".

Amongst its key **actions**, the Commission "urges Member States to ensure that access is a key objective of their information society strategies".

Installing the technology is not the major issue. The Information Society is not just about Information and Communication Technology. It is about social change. To make full use of the opportunities before us and, at the same time, to make Ireland a fairer and more inclusive society, we must build a society where lifelong learning becomes the norm. Continuous enhancement of the skills needed to navigate the maze of information will be an essential element in lifelong learning.

Most people will be impeded, as individuals, from access to information and access to Information and Communication Technology (ICT), not only by cost but also by a lack of awareness of the possibilities offered by the information society and by a lack of information-handling skills.

"rich in culture, learning and creativity"

Public libraries, locally organised and locally accountable, are very well placed to provide the access and support that people will need in a Learning Society. Which other agency is better equipped to be the vehicle for communities "rich in culture, learning and creativity" to embrace the Information Age?

With its tradition and ethos of universal access to its collections, the thrust of public libraries' input to this new society will continue to be to ensure that we do not have people who can be classed as information rich and others who can be classed as information poor.

"Libraries need to be ready, however, to adapt themselves to the opportunities and requirements of this new society"

Libraries need to be ready, however, to adapt themselves to the opportunities and requirements of this new society. Though libraries are ICT literate agencies, they are not fixated on ICT for its own sake. Libraries are concerned with the uses of information, with access and with democratic participation and countering social exclusion, and with placing ICT at the service of people.

4.3 The pillars of the public library service

There are three pillars to the public library service. It acts as a resource for Information and Learning, as a resource for Culture and the Imagination and as a resource for Children and Young People.

4.3.1 Public libraries as a resource for Information and Learning.

The public library bridges information gaps by providing accurate and up-to-date information for everyday living and problem solving and by providing a continually updated collection of reference works, in print and electronic form. It assists the development of its local community by providing information for business, and for community development, linking up, where relevant, with national and international information providers.

The library meets the public's right to know by providing information for dealing with everyday problems and citizen action information.

The library supports adult learners and education generally. In particular it supports action for adult literacy, supports adult independent learning, and supports persons undertaking distance education in practical ways by providing information, course materials and study space. It also assists people to develop the skills they need in a fast changing world, enhancing reading skills, ICT literacy, and general self-directed learning.

Snap Shot: *Libraries and the Information Age*

Tipperary Libraries Web site [www.iol.ie/~tip-plibs] has now been live for well over two years. It was described as "a splendid on-line resource", by Telecom Éireann when awarding the site a three star award earlier this year.

The main thrust of development has been focused on the County Tipperary Historical Society part of the site as this is the most heavily visited area. The Society's Web presence was specifically targeted at the foreign market, especially those with Tipperary roots in North America and Australia. Although the library helps out visitors as much as is possible from its Local Studies Department and refers them to the necessary sources in Ireland, the mail can, at times be overwhelming. Thus the site has developed, through necessity, into a central bulletin board where visitors post their genealogical research queries with their e-mail address and help each other out. The Web site has publicised the Local Studies Department extensively and visitors who are travelling to Ireland make a point of visiting the library as first port of call.

Future developments of the site will focus on developing the relationship with local educational facilities as they go on-line, both through the Schools and Children's Library Services and Local Studies in conjunction with the branches which will have public Web access.

4.3.2 Public libraries as a resource for Culture and the Imagination

The library promotes interest in literature, books and reading, and provides the materials for creative recreation by providing a continually updated collection of fiction and popular non-fiction books for lending, as well as audio-visual and multi-media materials.

"The library acts as the collective memory of the community"

The library acts as the collective memory of the community and the county/city by comprehensively collecting and making available local studies material of all types and by acting as a centre for local studies.

The library acts as a focal point of the living community, for social and cultural activities, being a point of contact for information on the arts, and providing space and assistance for literary, visual arts and community arts events.

The library supports literature in Irish, and Gaelic culture generally, providing a bi-lingual service to the public and promoting awareness of literature in Irish. It encourages reading in Irish amongst both children and adults and provides space and assistance for Irish language events.

Snap Shot: *Promoting Reading*

For a number of years, Cork City Library has organised activities for older people to broaden their reading experience. Such activities include establishing book clubs in most branch libraries, organising activities for older people and establishing contact with organisations involved with older people.

Adult book clubs add a new dimension to the pleasure of reading. They facilitate the coming together of older people with a love of reading and where literary activities can be organised by the members of the various clubs. There are six book clubs for older people in Cork City Library. The idea of a bookclub for older people originated in 1991 when a club was started in the Central Library. It was so successful that a second bookclub started in the Central Library and in a number of our branch libraries.

Initially, a member of library staff acts as a facilitator to organise the group but the underlying philosophy is that each club will determine what books, authors, themes they wish to discuss and what activities they wish to organise. Library staff act as facilitators and to support.

Membership is usually limited to 18 members and meetings are arranged on a monthly basis.

The activities of the bookclub include:
Review of books - all categories of material are included. It is for the members to decide.

- Discussion on writers - these can include local, national or international writers past or present.
- Talks and readings by writers either local or national. The Library co-operates with The Munster Literature Centre in organising talks and video presentations on Munster writers.
- Visits to places of literary or historical interest. Tours in the past have included Frank O'Connor's, Cork; Elizabeth Bowen country; Blasket Island writers; and the Irish Writers Museum.
- Social activities involving other book clubs.
- Interaction and exchanges between members of the bookclub and teenagers. This would include reminiscence sessions and activities such as table quizzes.

"The library acts as a centre for literacy and information skills, sharpening reading skills and assisting children to gain information through reading;"

4.3.3 Public libraries as a resource for Children and Young People

The library acts as a gateway to the world of knowledge for children, by providing books, multi-media materials and ICT resources to stimulate and improve their minds and imaginations;

The library acts as a centre for literacy and information skills, sharpening reading skills and assisting children to gain information through reading;

The library acts as a seedbed for culture by introducing children and young people to the world of arts and to the oral and material culture of their community.

Snap Shot: *Libraries and Children*

Cork City Library actively encourages children to become involved in reading from a very early stage. This is done in a number of ways:

- By organising special activities to draw attention to reading and books, and to build upon reading experiences. These include author visits, displays, library publications.
- By providing a forum for discussion on books and writers with children.
- By linking to schools and community groups.
- By making all children's libraries as aesthetically pleasing as possible and conveying a warm, welcoming atmosphere.
- By providing a wide and varied collection of reading material supplemented with non-book material such as talking books and CD-ROM packages.

Activities, displays and exhibitions designed to encourage and promote the skills of reading and writing among the younger community include:

- **Recommended reading lists and book displays**
Book displays on particular themes for different age groups are organised and in-house reading lists are compiled.
- **Storytime**
Weekly storytime and activity mornings are organised for younger readers.
- **Competitions**
Competitions are run on a regular basis either on a literary theme such as poetry, design a book cover, cartoons etc. or as part of special events such as World Book Day, National Tree Week etc.
- **Exhibitions**
Exhibitions are organised including selected authors, environmental issues and historical events such as 1798.
- **Library publications**
A number of children's libraries produce a library magazine at regular intervals. The magazine is compiled from material submitted by chil-

dren in the branch and includes articles, stories, poems, illustrations, book reviews and puzzles.

- **School visits**

Class visits are during school terms and include borrowing books, tours of the library, special events such as author readings.

- **Library skills course**

A library skills course is a recent innovation which is proving to be very popular with school visits. A specialised workbook accompanies the course with sections on fiction, non fiction, reference material, computer searching etc. The exercises also include demonstrating the facilities in specialised areas such as the local history collection.

- **Festivals**

A number of annual festivals are celebrated each year, including Children's Book Week where an extensive programme of events is organised each year.

4.4 From vision to results - the impact of the library service

4.4.1 Introduction

The public library service delivers vital services to a broad spectrum of people. It has done so for a long time and is in a strong position to continue for many years to come. It has had a strong social impact to date. With the growing importance of information and learning in society, coupled with the dangers of fragmentation, exclusion and marginalisation, the library service is in a strong position to have a greater impact into the future as it provides opportunities for everybody in society to make use of information, learning and culture to maximise their potential.

Again, this not something that has been confined to Ireland. All across the world, the value of public libraries is appreciated and its beneficial impact understood.

In 1997, the British Library Board published the results of research into the social impact of public libraries.[xi] This report notes the historical back-ground of public libraries. It states that "the founding of public libraries in the UK in the mid-nineteenth century was justified by the argument that they would have a major impact on social (or rather, anti-social) behaviour and attitudes. In particular they were seen as an effective way of luring workers away from public houses, criminal activities and the vice generally associated with urban industrialisation. Simultaneously, workers were expected through exposure to culture, to increase their skills and hence the overall level of skill in the labour market.... The two sides of public libraries are seen here: hand-in-hand with their controlling, civilising role, public libraries also performed a liberating function by providing the fast-expanding working and middle classes with self-instruction literature. Both aspects performed important social functions, hence Muddiman and Black's comment that : 'From its inception, therefore, the public library was called on to perform economic, tangible, utilitarian tasks'.

Regardless of its Victorian origins and the laudable, if patronising, values which suffused early libraries, it is undeniable that public libraries today continue to have a significant social impact. This was defined by the UK Department of National Heritage in the following terms:"Public libraries provide opportunities for learning, self-improvement, for business, the local community and in developing young people".[xii]

4.4.2 Scope of impact

The impact of the public library service is seen in many ways:

- The library acts as a point of access to new sources of information, particularly by allowing more equitable access to the Internet. The importance of equitable access to ICT resources is growing. As an increasing number of facilities: banking, shopping, using office equipment - rely on some level of ICT skills, a degree of ICT literacy is necessary in order to be able to participate in the mainstream of society. The role of the public library in providing access to ICT and to providing basic ICT literacy skills cannot be understated and free Internet access has recently been introduced to a small number of Irish public libraries.

Snap Shot : *Libraries-On-line*

Together with library sites in Limerick and Mayo, Dublin Corporation's branch library in Ballyfermot has become the European starting point for Microsoft Corporation's **LIBRARIES-ON-LINE programme**. The programme is a partnership that provides public internet and multi-media access in American and Canadian public libraries - and which is aimed particularly at redressing the problem of potential exclusion from the fast developing Information Society in areas of high unemployment and social deprivation.

LIBRARIES-ON-LINE in Ballyfermot provides free public access to an 8 PC LAN, equipped with internet access via ISDN lines, and a range of CD ROM based multi-media programmes. Since its launch by the Taoiseach in September 1997, public usage of the facility has consistently run at approximately 95%. The facilities provide hitherto unavailable free public access to a wide range of materials and information services for adults and children alike.

Apart from simply 'surfing the web' and accessing multi-media programmes, users in the library, construct their own web sites and set up their own E-mail addresses. This creates a real community awareness of the Information Society at the most accessible local level, in the public library. Perhaps most importantly, an opportunity is now in place whereby libraries and librarians can exercise a leading role in both developing , and in providing access to the Information Society.

Dublin Corporation regards the Ballyfermot **LIBRARIES-ON-LINE** facility as a model on which it proposes to base future library based developments as a key element in its strategy of empowering the citizens of Dublin through its information services.

- Public libraries act as **a support to business development.** They are in a position to provide information to all businesses but are particularly valuable to small, new businesses and to rural businesses. A survey of small businesses in the UK in 1996 identified that one of the main reasons that 75% of new companies fail is lack of information. New businesses are rarely in a position to buy information from private sources. Hence the need for public libraries to meet the need and make a direct contribution to economic development. In Ireland, this requirement is being met by the development of the South West Action Project (SWAP).

In rural areas, where enterprise is a vital component in maintaining the fabric of rural society, the role of the public library in providing access to information is even more vital.

Snap Shot: *South West Action Project in County Cork*

The South West Action Project (SWAP) commenced in 1995 and offers electronic access to business information to local SME's, local businesses and to individuals interested in enterprise. Many of these had previously probably not seen their local public library as being a relevant source of the specialist information they required.

The project was developed by Cork County and City Library services in partnership with An Chomhairle Leabharlanna, Forbairt and the County Enterprise Board.

Before SWAP, the provision of business information (almost exclusively in printed form) had proved to be:
- expensive - the initial and annual updating costs of books and directories;
- inefficient - the currency of information was always a source of suspicion in the case of printed sources;
- under-utilised - as part of the general refer-

ence service, it was not marketed as a distinct service or specifically targeted at a potential clientele.

Budgetary considerations meant that a comprehensive business reference collection could only be maintained at Library Headquarters in Cork City and in a county as large as Cork this had serious consequences for the potential user in peripheral regions of the county. The advent of information technology opened up new approaches to the delivery of business information services and SWAP has provided a new means of service provision.

The benefits of SWAP to both the library and the user can be summarised as:

- On-line availability of a wide range of information that can be accessed on demand.
- Searches can be tailored to the particular and specific needs of the client.
- The prompt delivery, by fax where applicable, of the information being sought.

Because the South West Action Project represented a new departure and a fresh start in business information provision by Cork County Library, it allowed the library to target new potential users and to market the service to a targeted audience. This marketing exercise has introduced to the public library a range of clients who would not have considered their local library had any potential to benefit or assist them in terms of their business enterprises and would only have seen it as providing recreational reading material or perhaps local history information. Such clients have been pleasantly surprised to discover that the public library can provide hard information as current as they could obtain elsewhere and with a rapidity of response equal to commercial information services. They have also been appreciative of the assistance that experienced library staff can provide in focusing their enquiries and in identifying likely avenues of information.

Library staff have played a key role in the implementation of the SWAP programme to-date. The introduction of new technology required the development of new skills and new approaches to the traditional 'reference interview' and the commitment and enthusiasm of staff have been essential components in selling the services and in its success. A complementary benefit of the SWAP programme has been its effect on users and on library staff in furthering the introduction of information technology in other areas of the library's reference service. Access to the Internet and to CD-ROM databases, an aspect of information provision introduced via SWAP, have become part of the library package in many centres, their introduction greatly facilitated by the experience gained by staff on the SWAP programme.

SWAP has proved a vehicle for advancing public library into a new era of service provision and for the user has offered a new perspective on the potential benefits that the library can provide, particularly in areas of service once considered beyond the scope of all but the largest municipal reference libraries.

After a pilot phase in County Cork, on-line business information services have now been implemented in counties Longford, Mayo, Roscommon, Waterford, Clare and in Dublin and Limerick City.

- By providing relevant information in an accessible manner, public libraries can form part of an **anti-poverty strategy**. A report on Russian libraries noted that "public libraries are now about the only places to offer free access to self-education and a pleasant pastime with cultural and intellectual treasures. Theatres, concerts, cinemas, museums, cultural centres, tourism - all these are hardly affordable for too many."[xiii] *The UK Comedia Report* concurs on the value of libraries for people in poverty and focuses on literacy: "In providing materials and events which encourage literacy, public libraries contribute to economic productivity. In this way, they are cheaper than policemen".[xiv]

- A 1994 report on US literacy amplifies this point: "As a nation [U.S.A.], we spend billions on education but even more on unemployment, welfare, police, prisons and jails. What we fail to provide for in the emerging literacy needs of our children, we pay for tenfold in the resulting myriad of social and educational problems directly relating from, or related to, the school failures of youth."[xv]

- The public library provides **a source of continuity**. Changes in the structure of the population are often accompanied by increased poverty and a sense of dislocation. Over the last decade, many parts of the world have seen increases in the proportion of elderly people, people from ethnic minority groups, unemployed people and people working in a flexible working market. The importance of public libraries in maintaining the quality of life in periods of social change has been noted. The library acts as an island of order, quiet and cleanliness, a haven in threatening times of change. The library meets a need for maintaining a sense of continuity, community and identity by sustaining and organising such activities as storytelling events, local literature competitions and providing material relevant to the local population.

- The Comedia Report argues that investing in people who underpin a community is critical in maintaining morale in contemporary society and is cheaper and more effective than anti-crime projects, custodial sentences and dealing with the effects of family breakdown.

- Public libraries contribute to the **development of town centres**. The location of libraries has a beneficial knock-on effect on surrounding commercial enterprises. *The Comedia Report* recorded that the importance of a new library opening went largely unnoticed by retailers, although there were many instances where local shops noticed increases in foot-fall and turnover. It also noted that property developers are increasingly aware of the potential of libraries for assisting struggling shopping centres. This is backed up by some evidence of libraries being included in general development proposals at peppercorn rents, a situation which also exists in Ireland.

- Public libraries have a direct **impact on the book-selling trade** in Ireland. Expenditure in excess of £4 million annually means that public libraries are the largest single purchaser of books in Ireland. Given that the range of books purchased is broad, the impact of library purchases on more specialist titles and on smaller, Irish, publishers is even more significant.

- The library acts as a **cultural meeting point**. In an increasingly multi-cultural society, libraries can provide cultural products for all sections of the community. Examples of important work in this area are to be found within the New Zealand public library service where services to the Chinese community have been developed and in Australia where improvements to collections have resulted in greater use of the library by Australian Aboriginals. As Irish society, and in particular Dublin society changes, the library can provide vital support services to individuals and groups from minority ethnic groups.

- In a wider definition of culture, the library also provides space for cultural works from, and for, a range of groups such as radical and minority political groups, minority lifestyles, minority interests, and people with disabilities.

- The library **supports the lifestyles of those not employed in the labour market**. The perception of the library as a safe, free space opens it up as a place for social interaction for those excluded from other areas.

- This means it is able to provide vital emotional support to groups such as women carers, volunteers, middle-aged unemployed men and elderly people. These groups are likely to be isolated and suffer financial hardship, hence their exclusion from other meeting places such as pubs, theatres, shops etc.

- Hartlepool library in the UK works extensively with unemployed people, providing information about job vacancies, offering basic literacy tuition and help with writing CVs. In the first 26 months that the service was offered, it resulted in 147 people being offered jobs.

Snap Shot: *Adult Literacy in Offaly and Limerick*

In 1994 the Department of Education and Science agreed to fund an action research project aimed at the promotion of literacy through the public library service. Part of the project was based in Offaly County Library, the other in Limerick City Library.

The project seeks to develop meaningful partnerships between the libraries and other stakeholders - literacy students, tutors, local literacy organisers and the National Adult Literacy Agency (NALA). The project presents the library as an active agent in literacy provision, promotes reading and makes a wide range of relevant books and audio-visual materials available to adult literacy students and their tutors, and generally promotes a reading culture.

Central to the success of the project has been this concept of partnership.

Many of the programmes were developed jointly by Offaly County and Limerick City Libraries, in conjunction with their respective literacy course organisers. The programmes include:

- library staff awareness training courses aimed at raising their awareness as to the problems literacy students face when contemplating joining the library;
- literacy tutor induction courses aimed at promoting the stock and services of the library to tutors and, through them, to their students;
- literacy students induction courses aimed at introducing the library staff and services to students and encouraging use of the library;
- advertising and promotion of the library services and literacy schemes.

Offaly County Library established a computer learning facility in Tullamore Branch Library with a number of multi-media based literacy aids (e.g. the New Reading Disk). It was recognised that multi-media applications have an important part to play in the teaching of basic skills such as literacy and numeracy. It was also felt that involvement with information technology within the general library environment would provide a boost to the students self-confidence and would encourage further interaction with other library services.

Limerick City Library also provided a computer learning facility - although neither facilities are limited to basic skills tuition.

- The library acts **a gateway for health information.** Some health information is available from public libraries. This may be related to specific illnesses or diseases or in the form of a health directory, aimed at sign-posting how to find health information. The Help for Health project in the south-west of England estimates that around 30,000 enquiries were received during 1995/6 from a catchment population of 6 million. In Ireland, a survey carried out by the Library Association of Ireland in 1995, in co-operation with the Department of Health and Children, has shown that there are serious deficiencies in access, awareness and availability of information for both healthcare staff and patients in Ireland. A simultaneous study of international best practice has shown that professional library and information services have the ability to provide cost-effective and timely access to relevant information in the required format.

To remedy the deficiency, a 1998 Consumer Health Information research project[xvi] has recommended that public libraries should form partnerships or co-operative agreements with health sciences libraries. In addition, a designated librarian should be responsible for Consumer Health Information in each library authority and should develop more formal co-operation with the voluntary sector and improve access for those with special needs.

4.5 A future for the public library service

The project team believes the case for public libraries has been proven many times and in many countries. It is happy that the public library service is delivering a valuable service in Ireland to-day. However, the project team is in no way complacent. It recognises that there are serious deficiencies in the Irish public library service.

The project team believes that the library service has been stifled in delivering the best service it can by a lack of investment in infrastructure, stock and staff.

It has also been hampered by a lack of awareness by the public of the range of services available through the library. This lack of awareness has been allowed linger too long by librarians taking a timid approach to marketing their services.

In some areas too, the library service has not been oriented to meet the needs of library users as it should be. This is evidenced in areas such as unsuitable opening hours and inflexibility. A fuller picture of the current state of the service is outlined in the next chapter of this report.

The project team believes that the time has come for a sea-change in the approach of local and central government to the public library service, which must be accompanied by a renewed sense of purpose by the library service itself.

This report sets out the first steps that must be taken to implement such a change. If implemented properly, the library can retake its place as a central and dynamic public service which contributes to the welfare and development of the entire community. The library service has the potential to become a centre of light and learning in every community in Ireland.

The project team believes that the commitment is there to realise this potential and that a renewed partnership between all the stakeholders in the public library service will start to build the library service of the future. The project team envisions the future library service as having the following characteristics:

"The project team believes that the library service has been stifled in delivering the best service it can by a lack of investment in infrastructure, stock and staff."

- It will have a clear vision of its own future.
- It will be a repository for cultural materials of all kinds - books, CDs, CD-ROM's, periodicals, multimedia etc..
- It will be a welcoming space, equally accessible to all social groups.
- It will have extensive and versatile opening hours.
- It will be staffed by suitably qualified and trained personnel.
- It will be a gateway to other local authority and government services.
- It will be a supporter of education and learning at many levels.
- It will be a centre for cultural activities.
- It will be an active partner of the community and a centre of community awareness and activity.
- It will operate from a purpose-designed building in urban areas, designed from the inside out. Its form will follow its function.
- It will be fully-equipped with information and communication technology, providing access to ICT for the public.
- It will have on-line access 24 hours per day.
- It will raise part of its own funding.

4.6 Conclusion

The public library serves the public well. Its role, although unsung, is important. Changes in society, in demography and in information provision underline the continuing importance of libraries. Nevertheless, there is a need for libraries to change and improve their services. The changes and improvements will be designed to serve the customer and the community better and must focus on giving greater and more equitable access to an enhanced service.

Notes

ii   *Irish Marketing Surveys: Omnibus Research Into Use of Libraries, November 1997.*

iii   *Opening of Boyle Library, February 1998*

iv   *Speech at opening of Galway Library Extension.*

v   *Out of Hours: a study of economic, social and cultural life in twelve town centres in the UK.; Comedia and Calouste-Gulbenkian Foundation, London, 1991*

vi   *Better Local Government, A Programme for Change, Department of the Environment, Dublin, December 1996 p.95*

vii   *In "European Voice" 14-19 May 1998, based on speech at conference organised by the Centre for Economic Performance, London*

viii   *Information Society Ireland - Strategy for Action, Forfas, December 1996, p iii.*

ix   *"Building the Information Society: Moving Canada into the 21st Century"; Information Highway Advisory Council Secretariat, Canada, 1996*

x   *The Social and Labour Market Dimension of the Information Society. People First - The Next Steps; European Commission, Directorate-General for Employment, Industrial relations and Social Affairs, March 1998.*

xi   *The Social Impact of Public Libraries: A Literature Review, Evelyn Kerslake & Margaret Kinnel, British Library Research and Innovation Centre, 1997*

xii   *Reading the Future, 1997, p4*

xiii   *Kuzmin E., "Russian libraries in the context of social, political and economic and political reforms", IFLA Journal, 21(2), 1995*

xiv   *Comedia, Borrowed Time? The future of public libraries in the UK, Stroud, Comedia, 1993.*

xv   *Talan C.S., Family Literacy makes sense: Families that read together, succeed together, The Bottom Line 7(3/4), 1994*

xvi   *Well Read: Developing Consumer Health Information Services in Ireland, Jennifer MacDougall/Library Association of Ireland, 1998*

five

Libraries Today

5

5.1. Introduction

This chapter sets out a high-level assessment of where Irish public libraries are today, in the opinion of the project team.

The purpose of this chapter is to provide a template for the analysis of the issues set out later in the report and to provide a background for the recommendations that are made. It can also be used as a basis for comparison with other sectors and other library services.

5.2. What services do public libraries provide?

There is a core of library services that all libraries provide, consisting of the lending of books and other materials, as well as providing access to reference and information services. In addition, each library authority provides a local studies section which focuses on material produced within the authority's area or about that area. Individual local studies sections each contain material of high historical, literary and commercial value. Collectively, they comprise a resource of great national and indeed international importance.

At either branch or library authority level, most authorities are involved in activities such as lectures, exhibitions or educational courses in a wide range of topics. The scale, frequency and nature of these activities varies between library authorities.

"In 1998, local authorities will spend approximately £36 million of their resources in providing the service."

The library also participates in numerous projects alongside other agencies and organisations where the resources of the library are considered useful to the project and where the subject is considered to be relevant to library users and potential users.

5.3. Basic facts about the public library service

There are 318 public libraries in Ireland[xvii]. In addition there are a further 949 service points in operation, which include mobile libraries, hospitals, schools, day-care centres etc. Altogether, the public library service employs approximately 1,300 people. In 1998, local authorities will spend approximately £36 million of their resources in providing the service. In addition, the Department of the Environment and Local Government will invest slightly over £3 million of National Lottery funds in library infrastructure.

The Minister for Education and Science supports the development of libraries in primary schools by way of an annual book grant. In 1998 this is estimated to be almost £1 million. This funding is administered by Library Authorities.

"a total library membership of about 850,000 people"

These resources, totalling about £40 million are used to deliver a service to the public that has the following characteristics:

In terms of **usage:**

- The average rate of library membership, nationally, is 24%. This implies a total library membership of about 850,000 people.

- Many non-members also use the library. The first national marketing survey on libraries, carried out in November 1997, indicated that 32% of the adult population use public libraries.[xviii]

- Research in a number of library authorities, for example in Clare County Library, has shown that for every item issued in a larger service point, there is an equivalent recorded use of the reference and information facilities.

- There are disparities within the global figure of 32% usage. For example, the use of the library by urban-dwellers is 34% while the usage by rural dwellers is 27%. There is also evidence that farmers (as opposed to rural-dwellers) have particular difficulties in accessing library services. Likewise the larger urban authorities and larger towns in mainly rural authority areas show above average membership, while rural areas lag well behind

In terms of **service** delivery:

- 38% of branch libraries are open to the public for 30 hours or more per week. 16% are open between 20 and 30 hours per week. 46% are open fewer than 20 hours per week. The trend in recent years has been towards better opening hours.

- Those branches that open for longer hours offer a wider range of services and tend to be in larger urban authorities and in larger population centres in otherwise rural authority areas.

- In addition to branch libraries, the other service points, which generally hold small collections, are available for fewer hours generally than branch libraries and are managed by temporary, part-time staff or volunteers.

- In addition to book-lending and general reference, libraries provide services in the following areas:

  - Adult literacy programmes and family literacy programmes.
  - Open and distance learning programmes.
  - Exhibitions and talks on community-based development.
  - Children's summer projects.
  - Tuition in Information and Communication Technology.
  - Exhibitions by local voluntary groups in the library premises.
  - Co-operation with local businesses to provide training materials for job-seekers.
  - Placements in the library for job-seekers, physically disabled and the mentally handicapped.

In addition, libraries are a local outlet for:

- Government and EU publications
- Government and EU information campaigns
- Planning information
- Information on local authority services and events
- Information on social welfare entitlements,
- Careers development information,
- Information on educational opportunities,
- Information on community groups and initiatives

In terms of **structure**:

- The Minister for the Environment and Local Government has overall responsibility for the library service at national level. As such, he or she enacts, and keeps under review, the legislation underpinning the system and formulates national policy relating to the service.

- Library authorities, of which there are 32 country-wide, are responsible for the day-to-day management and control of public libraries. Library authorities are generally synonymous with local authorities (County Councils and County Boroughs). Two exceptions are Tipperary and Galway where, in each case, two local authorities combine to act as a library authority.

- An Chomhairle Leabharlanna (The Library Council) is a semi-state body under the aegis of the Department of the Environment and Local Government. It comprises a Council of 12 members drawn equally from the library and local government sectors, with an independent Chairman. Its role is to advise the Minister for the Environment and Local Government and library authorities on library matters. It also promotes library co-operation.

5.4 Service delivery in branches

Each library authority is responsible for delivering the library service in its own area. Accordingly, there is not a standard and uniform service delivered countrywide. Local conditions, both positive and negative, contribute to a service which is of a variable standard and divergent range, both within and between library authorities. There is little statistical information at national level on the operations of libraries at branch level. However, in preparing Library Development Programmes, approximately one third of library branches provided a branch profile. In addition, in 1998 a survey of branch libraries was carried out as part of the National Policy on Libraries and Information Services. Between the two of these sources the following general findings can be deduced:

- In terms of usage, 40% of libraries issue fewer than 3 books per head of population in their catchment area per year.

- The penetration of computerisation for house-keeping functions (catalogues, circulation etc.) within those branch libraries was found to be just over 40%.

- 20 out of 32 library authorities provide computers for public usage. These are mainly used to access CD-ROM's. Other uses include Internet access, word-processing and spreadsheets. There is not a standard approach to the supply of computers, their operation or functionality amongst library authorities. Nor is it possible to state the level of penetration of computers throughout each library authority branch network although it is noted that 12% of branches surveyed in 1998 offer Internet access to their users.

- Almost half the service points profiled are less than 100m² in size. Only 6 are more than 600m²

Snap Shot: *Purpose built library - Tallaght, Co. Dublin*

At 1,900 m², Tallaght County Library is one of the biggest libraries in the country. It opened its doors on the 14th December, 1994 and serves 70,000 people.

Centrally located in the new town of Tallaght, the library also forms part of the local authority civic offices and is an integral and valued element in the delivery of the Council's policy of social inclusion and of accessibility.

The library was purpose built to the highest standards and is open 52 hours per week. It delivers an innovative, pro-active and efficient service through its eleven members of staff.

The purpose built nature of the library means that it performs excellently under the following headings:

Space:
The design of the library building reflects an image of openess, and of space. The county library is spacious, relaxed and informal, emphasising the role of the library as a cultural and recreational facility.

Location:
Location is without doubt the prime benefit of the library. The decision to build the library in the hub of the local authority administrative structure as well as in the heart of the retail area of the county means that the service is convenient to library users.

Access:
The library is housed on one level which allows for:
- accessibility for disabled users;
- security/supervision and
- service delivery from a single control desk.

Snap Shot: Conversion of existing building to a library - Dunshaughlin Co. Meath

A part-time library service had been provided in Dunshaughlin since the 1930's. No specially designated premises had ever been in use prior to the opening of the converted St. Patrick's Church premises in September, 1996.

When the decision was made by Meath County Council to provide a library service which would more adequately meet the needs of the growing population, the choice of premises was of crucial importance. The choice lay in providing a purpose built facility or converting the old St. Patrick's Church. This building was of inadequate size to cope with the increase in population but was in reasonable physical condition, having been in use until a larger church was built in the early 1980's.

A number of factors contributed to the decision to opt for the use of a converted church premises as the location for the new library:

The location in an accessible site in the centre of the village made it an appropriate one for library use. The mature grounds on which the building was sited provided an attractive setting, a factor not readily available with a new building;

Meath County Council already owned the building;

The structural condition of the building was good and it had been well maintained while in use;

The architectural quality of the building, especially its impressive stone facade and attractive internal features, made it worthy of preservation;

The premises had adequate space to meet the needs of the population.

The refurbished building was opened to the public in September 1996 and has been successfully operating since. Registration numbers for December 1997 show a figure of 2812 which represents over 30% of the catchment population. This contrasts with a 5% figure in 1991. Annual issues at December, 1997 were 43,358, a seventeen fold increase over the 1991 figure.

The character of the old church has been maintained and some features are still in use. For example, the raised altar area, is now used for lectures, class and other group visits, art and writers' workshops and the mounting of art exhibitions. A strong local art group has been making especially effective use of this area for their frequent exhibitions. The church gallery is also in use as an arts administration centre for the Arts Officers.

The architectural and functional merits of the premises have been recognised at national and international level. The library was awarded 2nd Prize in the An Taisce Ellison Award for Environmental Excellence in 1996. It was shortlisted for the Public Library Building Awards 1997, a U.K. and Irish list of refurbished library premises and awarded a 'highly recommended' status.

5.5. Who uses libraries?

The IMS survey referred to earlier made the following findings in relation to public libraries:

- The response to a question concerning the frequency of using public libraries is as follows:

Weekly:	6%
Fortnightly:	8%
Monthly:	10%
Other:	8%
Never:	68%

- An analysis of the 32% of the population who use libraries shows that in terms of social class, 45%

are in the ABC1 category, 24% in DE, 23% in C2 and only 9% in category, F - Farmers.

- In terms of age-profile, the breakdown is as follows

15-24:	27%
25-34:	18%
35-49:	29%
50-64:	16%
65 +:	10%

- It is important to note that the survey did not sample anyone under the age of 15.

- In terms of regional distribution, 35% of users live in Dublin, 27% in Munster, 21% in the rest of Leinster and 17% in Connacht/Ulster. This is broadly in line with the distribution of population generally, although the proportion of library-users in Dublin is slightly higher than its proportion of the population.

- While libraries are generally open to all and are seen as one of the more accessible services provided by the state, there are still a number of barriers that may prevent people from availing of the service.

Factors which may prevent greater take-up of the service include:

- the quality of service;
- the quality of the infrastructure, including book-stock;
- the location of library buildings;
- the level and structure of library charges;
- the number and scheduling of opening hours;
- difficulties with physical access for some potential users;
- literacy difficulties and language difficulties for some potential users;
- the perception of the library service by some potential users.

"There are approximately 11.16 million stock items in the library system in Ireland."

These issues are discussed in more detail in Chapter 6 of this report.

5.6. What material is available in public libraries?

There are approximately 11.16 million stock items in the library system in Ireland. These are categorised as follows:

Adult Non-fiction	3.51 million
Adult Fiction	2.43 million
Children's	3.10 million
Schools	1.85 million
Non-Book Materials	0.27 million

(CDs, Tapes, Talking Books, Photographic, Maps, Art etc.)

In addition, public libraries have subscriptions to over 3,500 periodicals.

Other items can be obtained on loan from public libraries in the UK and from the British Library. In 1996, the last year for which complete figures are available, a total of 13.17 million items were issued by public libraries. These are categorised as follows:

Adult Non-fiction	2.96 million
Adult Fiction	4.92 million
Children's	4.69 million
Non-Book Materials	0.60 million

These figures do not take account of school library usage.

Loan periods are almost evenly divided. 15 library authorities allow a loan period of 2 weeks and 15 allow a period of 3 weeks. There are also limits to the number of items that may be borrowed at any one time, ranging from 2 to 6.

All library authorities charge for the overdue return of borrowed items. 27 of the 32 authorities charge £0.20 per item per week, or less. 11 library authorities also charge for reserving books. These range from £0.20 to £0.50 with the majority charging the postage costs of notifying members of the availability of the reserved item.

When an item is not available in one library authority, it may be borrowed from another or through larger institutions such as the British Library. It is a system that has a lot of potential but relies on the cooperation of the lending library and the wide availability of catalogue information.

Inter-library loans are often slow and are time-consuming on the part of library staff. Some categories of book are also excluded from such loans for reasons that now appear outdated. Inter-library loans are expensive for the library authority. According to Ameritech[xix], inter-library loans in 1995 amounted to 132,000. An assumed cost of £5.00 per request gives an overall cost of £660,000. The charge to the public for an inter-library loan varies widely. 22 library authorities charge for such loans. Over half of these charge £3.00 or over per item. Some charge the postage cost, as for reservations.

5.7. How are public libraries marketed?

In general, libraries have a reasonable approach to the local promotion of activities and events. However, there is little promotion of the core services of libraries and no national promotion of the library service. One of the few examples of a national marketing initiative is the annual Children's Book Festival, held each Autumn. It is considered to be very successful.

Other marketing measures, i.e. the presentation of library services in the best possible light, varies considerable from authority to authority and from branch to branch. In some branches and authorities, marketing efforts and marketing potential are undermined by the poor quality of the service available.

5.8. What are the staffing levels?

50% of library staff work in the 6 largest library authorities.[xx] In overall terms, there is one professional librarian for every 1.30 service points. However, within the different categories of library authority, large and mid-size authorities have one professional member of staff between 2 service points, while in the smallest and largest authorities, the situation is somewhat better.

"there is little promotion of the core services of libraries and no national promotion of the library service"

The survey of branch libraries in 1998 revealed that 42% of library staff are professionally qualified librarians, although not all were employed in professional grades. The average length of service in the library was 16.5 years.

The sole recognised professional school in librarianship which operates in Ireland is that in UCD. It offers a one-year post-graduate diploma in Library and Information Studies and a one-year full-time, or two-year part-time, Masters Degree. It also offers library and information studies as part of a Social Science Degree. Distance-learning is available for all grades, including through UK colleges.

In-service training for library staff tends to be better developed in larger authorities. Specialist training and development is provided through the Library Association, by the sections within the association, and by An Chomhairle Leabharlanna. This tends to be of a more ad hoc nature rather than as part of a training programme. Formal training for para-professional grades is rare.

5.9. How good is the Information and Communication Technology infrastructure?

24 library authorities have contracts with vendors of Library Management Systems. The contracts are with different vendors and some libraries have more complete automation than others. Automation has not yet been implemented in many of the branches of authorities whose headquarters operations have been automated. The fixed cost of automating a library authority is high, with the basic cost for software, catalogue data and host computer remaining constant. There is no system in place for sharing of automated catalogue data although An Chomhairle Leabharlanna is working towards achieving one.

The library authorities which have yet to automate are generally small or mid-size and the cost per user of implementing automation is disproportionately high.

5.10 How good is the stock in libraries?

There are approximately 11.16 million items of stock held by libraries. Approximately £4.6 million will be spent on stock in 1998 which, at an average cost of £25 per item suggests that in excess of 180,000 new items will be purchased. However, public libraries hold some stock which is quite old and worn. The level of investment and consequently the quality and range of stock varies between library authorities. Indeed, there appears to be a link between the level of investment in stock and the level of usage of the library. Therefore, the library authority bookfund is taken to be a useful indicator of investment in the library service.

A per capita assessment for 1998 shows the lowest estimated bookfund to be £0.29 and the highest to be £3.18. The national average is £1.27. These figures do not include expenditure financed by grant aid received from the Department of Education and Science for primary schools library books. With the average cost of a book being about £25, it is clear that library authorities investing sums as low as 29p per person - or 1 book between 86 people - are going to have difficulties in maintaining an attractive level and quality of stock. This has implications for the level of membership and the quality of service being offered to the public.

5.11 How free are public libraries ?

Under the 1983 Local Government (Financial Provisions)(No. 2) Act, library authorities are allowed to charge for a wide range of services, including library services. The decision on whether to charge and the level, scope and exemptions of such a charge are decided by the library authority and neither the Minister nor the Department have a role.

Research carried out by the Library Association of Ireland suggests that there is a linkage between the introduction of library charges and library member-ship and issues. However, on the basis of the available data, it is difficult to be conclusive about this. Certainly, the introduction of charges in the mid-1980s was accompanied by a dip in membership and issues. However, during the same period there were also cutbacks in opening hours and in book-funds. Accordingly, it is not possible to be definitive in ascribing the introduction of charges as the cause of a decline in usage of the library service at that time.

5.12. Summary

The public library service is a local service with significant presence in Irish life. It has over 1,000 points of presence in all parts of the country.

Total funding of the library service amounts to about £40 million per annum. A large majority of the funding (90%) of the library service comes from library Authorities.

There is significant variation in the investment levels in the library service. This results in the quality of infrastructure and levels and quality of service supplied by library authorities. This in turn has implications for the level of membership which, nationally, stands at approximately 850,000.

In general terms, recent years have seen an overall increase in investment in the library service by library authorities, but the increases are on a low base.

There are significant variations in the availability of information and communication technology and in the range and quality of book stock.

The current supply of capital is insufficient to meet the expressed demand for library investment. This demand is measured by library proposals on hands, research carried out by An Chomhairle Leabharlanna and by the LAI report "Public Libraries 2000".

Notes

xvii   Unless otherwise stated, statistical information in this chapter is supplied by An Chomhairle Leabharlanna or the Department of Environment and Local Government.

xviii   IMS Omnibus Survey, November 1997. A sample 1400 adults were surveyed concerning their usage of and attitude to public libraries.

xix   In a submission to the project.

xx   Ranked by population.

six

Views on the Public
Library Service

6

6.1 Introduction

This chapter contains a summary of views and opinions concerning public libraries today that are within the terms of reference of this project and which have been expressed during this project. These views were obtained through:

- submissions received from members of the public and from interested groups and organisations;

- documentary information on research in the library sector and on similar initiatives in Ireland and overseas;

- views expressed by the project team itself, based upon its experience in the library and local government sector;

- the outcome of consultations with key individuals and groups.

The project team believes that a response to the views expressed in relation to the public library service must also take account of the changes that are underway in a number of sectors. These changes would be less obvious to library-users but are vital in framing a national policy on public libraries. These changes are occurring in:

- Local Government, where radical change in how it conducts its business is underway;

- Information and Communication Technology (ICT), where an explosion in information sources and in technology is transforming society;

- Irish society, where the way people live their lives is also changing rapidly;

- Efforts to improve social inclusion through initiatives such as the National Anti-Poverty Strategy.

6.2 Submissions

6.2.1 Who made submissions?

The first comment to be made is that the overall number of submissions received by the project team indicates that there is considerable interest in the library service amongst individual members of the public and amongst groups and organisations.

794 submissions were received from members of the public and from interested groups and organisations. However, 355 of these were concerned with the provision of a library at one location, leaving 439 submissions of general interest.

Of these, 350 were received from individuals. Many of these submissions started by praising their local library before suggesting where improvements could be made. They also recognised the potential which public libraries have to meet their needs.

The other 89 submissions received were from a mixture of local and national organisations, of a voluntary, commercial or representative nature. They unanimously endorsed the role of the library as a service which aids their development.

A copy of the advertisement placed in national and local newspapers, seeking submissions is included as Appendix I

6.2.2 What did the submissions say?

(a)   Individuals
Many individual submissions raised more than one issue and some were very comprehensive indeed.

Most of the submissions, not surprisingly, were based on the individual experience of the correspondent's local library. In several cases, this was compared with library services in other countries or in other parts of Ireland.

The submissions were generally concerned with improving the service, and while several recognised the cost of such improvements, very few submissions suggested where this funding might be found.

In order to assess the response from individuals, policy issues raised have been placed in 11 categories. The 4 categories with most entries are as follows:

- **Better stock:**
  This includes calls for improvements in: quality and quantity of books, research, reference, historical and archival publications, magazines/periodicals, indexing of stock, videos/tapes, audio books.

- **Better infrastructure:**
  This includes calls for the provision of a new library or refurbishment of an existing one; provision or upgrade of a mobile library; improvement of interior/exterior of library; additional facilities: toilets, cafes, language-learning facilities.

- **Better opening hours:**
  This includes calls for longer opening hours; better scheduling; late-night and week-end opening; more flexible opening; more activities.

- **More Information and Communication Technology (ICT):**
  This includes calls for more computers; Internet access; on-line information access, on-line catalogues; on-line ordering of books; more CD-ROMs.

These four categories form the framework within which the project team addressed the policy issues and structured its recommendations.

A summary categorisation of all issues mentioned in submissions is set out in the table below:

Category	No. of References
Better Stock	167
Better Infrastructure	395*
Better Opening Hours	113
More Information Technology	108
More Furniture and Equipment	47
Better Facilities for Children/Schools	46
Better Staffing Levels	31
Better Information and Education Services	30
Changes in Charges\Fines	26
Better Image	20
Changes in Membership System	5
Total	988

* Includes 272 submissions seeking library at a specific location.

While there was a broad consensus about the approach to particular issues, it must be noted that not all the submissions were in agreement. For example:

- Many people wished for libraries to be the centres of activity and learning - a few wanted them to be quiet places of study.

- Most people were in favour of greater use of IT - a small number were against this development.

- Several people indicated that they were against library charges - others were in favour of charges and in particular were willing to pay for enhanced services, such as Internet access.

A list of individuals who made submissions is at Appendix II

(b) Organisations

The project team was encouraged by the fact that 89 organisations made submissions to its work. The team was particularly impressed that the range of organisations making the effort to participate in the project was so wide. They included national and local organisations and ranged from archaeological societies to literacy schemes and from enterprise boards to anti-poverty groups. While their backgrounds were diverse, most of the submissions recognised the value of the public library service and sought improvements to meet the particular needs of their members or target group. These included provision of better physical access for people with disabilities, better Irish-language services, provision of music-rooms, better information and material in a range of subject-areas.

A brief summary of some submissions of particular interest is set out below.

- **Information Society Commission**

  The Information Society Commission recognises the access to information and learning provided by libraries to people outside the formal education system.

It cites the Libraries On-line Programme[xxi] as a good example of a partnership approach resulting in enhanced facilities and calls for it to be extended.

The Commission recognises that more resources are required to enable libraries to maximise their potential as information centres and the Commission will actively promote awareness of the role that public libraries can play in a Learning Information Society.

"more resources are required to enable libraries to maximise their potential as information centres"

The Commission recommends that an ISDN Internet connection be provided for every library in the country. It also recommends that all citizens should have access to e-mail via the public library system by the year 2000.

- **Combat Poverty Agency**

Combat Poverty recommends that the policy review should adopt the principles of the National Anti-Poverty Strategy and a social rights approach to public service delivery. In particular, resources should be targeted at areas of greatest need.

Combat Poverty recommends that libraries should be open to flexible and innovative ways of providing an accessible and inclusive service.

It also recommends that libraries should develop 5 year local service plans and targets through a consultative process with the local community.

Combat Poverty recognises the role the library has in supporting education at all levels, formal and informal, and from pre-school to continuing or second chance education.

It asks that the policy group examine how public libraries can complement or link to local authori-

ty "one-stop-shops". It also recommends that libraries expand their involvement in the arts and reiterates the call from the Information Society Commission that libraries should be local access centres to electronic information for citizens.

- **Library Association of Ireland (LAI) (City and County Librarians Branch).**

Education and Literacy
The LAI seeks an endorsement from the Government of the public library's key role in education and literacy.

It asks that the role of the public library in the provision of a school library service - both primary and secondary should be defined and properly funded.

It calls for adequate resources to ensure a quality materials collection in each library service

Information
It calls for a Government commitment to its information policy with a central role for public libraries by:

"Combat Poverty recommends that libraries should be open to flexible and innovative ways of providing an accessible and inclusive service."

setting up a task force to advise on channelling public information through the library network;

making a funding commitment to implement the task force findings;

giving responsibility for procuring EU funding for ICT to An Chomhairle Leabharlanna.

It urges an ICT training strategy for library staff and calls for a programme to digitise all catalogues and local history/special collections in public libraries, with Internet access to same.

Arts, Culture & Heritage

The LAI calls for an endorsement of the leading role of the County/City Librarian in developing the Arts, Cultural and Heritage policy and strategy of local authorities. It also calls for the role of the library service as a focal point in this area to be recognised and supported.

Recreation

The LAI recommends that new library buildings should include provision for amenities and facilities such as public toilets, public telephones and refreshment facilities.

Customer Service

The LAI recommends that a priority of the policy should be making libraries free, open and accessible to all.

It calls for a more flexible staffing structure to allow for extended opening hours.

National Policy / National Commitment

The LAI calls for the National Policy to be accepted by Government and to be coupled with a National Commitment. The commitment should use as its base, the Library Authority Development Programmes. A capital investment programme should be put in place which gives priority to addressing "blackspots" in public library provision; to ensuring that each library authority has at least one "Centre of Excellence" and to providing 100% funding for automation.

Role of An Chomhairle Leabharlanna

The LAI recommends that the membership of An Chomhairle should be reconstituted to reflect its primary role. It urges that An Chomhairle should work as a public relations vehicle and as an active research source for the public library service.

The LAI recommends that An Chomhairle be charged with sourcing funding for the public library service at national and EU levels.

The LAI calls on the Department of Environment and Local Government to raise its financial contribution to An Chomhairle to at least the level of local authority funding.

Staffing

The LAI recommends access to continuing professional education for County/City Librarians. It also calls for further work in this area to be jointly carried by An Chomhairle and the LAI.

It also calls on the Government to put in place a Human Resource Management Policy at national level.

- **National Adult Literacy Agency (NALA)**

NALA identifies the scope that libraries have to contribute to local initiatives aimed at tackling problems associated with low literacy skills.

NALA recognises that fear of ICT may lead to further exclusion of disadvantaged groups and calls for a level playing pitch for all citizens in terms of access to the information society as it develops.

It recommends improved marketing of the variety of educational/ cultural activities taking place in libraries.

It calls for the development of the relationship between the public library service and local literacy schemes and for literacy awareness training for library staff. Likewise, NALA calls for library induction programmes for literacy tutors and students.

NALA also calls for extended opening hours and greater access to ICT.

- **National Archives**

The National Archives is concerned at the slow rate of progress in the provision of local authority archives services.

It recommends that future developments in library policy should take account of local authorities' statutory obligation towards their archives.

It recommends that archives and library services should be developed in conjunction with each other and in a manner that permits the full development of each. It calls for separate and additional financial provision for archives services.

- **International Education Services (IES) (Booksellers)**

IES, a commercial company, makes the point that the library service is the largest information infrastructure in the country. It adds that, whereas adequate funding for the development of arts and culture has been made in recent years, the library service has not kept pace. It points to the incongruity of a recent survey which showed that 60% of the population use public libraries while 3% use arts centres.

IES recommends that a schools library service be extended to second-level schools. It also warns against the direct funding of schools libraries as teachers are not equipped or trained properly on children's literature or on book selection.

IES is worried that direct funding of schools libraries will lead to a narrow range of books and that schools will become a target of remainder merchants. It states that the public library service has the infrastructure and qualified personnel to ensure that the best material is made available to schools.

IES advises that for every £50,000 spent on books, a new job is created in the Irish booktrade. Adequate library funding ensures that the booktrade remains a vibrant industry.

IES also calls for increased capital and current funding of libraries.

A list of organisations that made submissions is also included at Appendix II

"for every £50,000 spent on books, a new job is created in the Irish booktrade"

6.3 Summary of issues

It is worth stating that most of the issues raised in the submissions and consultations did not come as a surprise to the project team. The same issues had also been raised in discussion within the team during the research phase of the project.

Taking into account all of the submissions, documentary research, discussions within the project team itself and consultations with other parties, the project team believes that the following 10 issues are the most relevant ones to determining the future of the public library service:

- The need for a clear focus and direction for the public library service.

- The need to deliver a better library service to meet changes in Irish society by:

  Developing enhanced opening hours;
  Investing in library staff;
  Improving equality of access to library services;
  Improving specialised services;
  Improving libraries information services;
  Developing life-long learning services.

- The need to provide adequate infrastructure - a network of modern, properly equipped and staffed service points covering the entire country that will ensure libraries play a key role in the information society.

- The need to develop new service-delivery methods that will enable areas of low population and other isolated communities to have equal access to library services in a cost-efficient manner.

- The need to improve the range and quality of stock.

- The need to improve local and national marketing of library services.

- The need to improve co-operation with other library and non-library organisations and for libraries to play a full role in the process of local government reform.
- The need to improve schools library services.

- The need to maintain the library as a centre of culture.

- The need to improve the service through library research.

All of these have implications for the type of library service that will be provided into the future. Regardless of whether these changes are seen as opportunities or threats, it is clear that libraries will have to change themselves in order to optimise their contribution to the development of Irish society.

This report is seen as a first step towards addressing the first issue by providing a clear focus and direction for the public library service. The remaining 9 issues are discussed in the next chapter of this report. It also contains recommended actions to be taken by Government Departments, An Chomhairle Leabharlanna and library authorities.

Notes

xxi *Libraries On-line is an initiative of Microsoft, in association with other ICT companies to provide internet access to public libraries. It has been implemented on a pilot basis in Ireland, in 5 libraries.*

seven

7

Policy Issues & Recommendations

In this chapter the project team reviews the key policy issues for public library development and suggests steps that might be taken. It also makes recommendations across a wide range of issues. The Terms of Reference for the policy review indicate that the Minister for the Environment and Local Government should be the focus for recommendations by the project team. It is clear however, that if the library service is going to develop, it will require an input from all the stakeholders in the service. Accordingly, some of the recommendations outlined below are addressed to other players in the public library service.

The project team believes that a continued and enhanced partnership will be required from everybody if we wish to see a worthwhile, dynamic and forward looking library service.

This is the key issue for the project team. The objective of public libraries is to deliver a service to the public. All other objectives are secondary and subsidiary. To meet this objective, the service must be available, accessible, comprehensive and of a high quality.

Delivery of such a service raises many related issues, some of which are discussed below.

"it is ridiculous that the library should be closed all day on Monday and every lunchtime!"

7.1.1 Developing enhanced opening hours:

The project team is satisfied that significant improvements in the availability of library services are necessary. This will be most obviously achieved through a programme of enhanced opening hours. Many of the submissions received by the project team spoke of library members being unable to visit the library during lunchtime or at week-ends. One submission put the case strongly by stating that "it is ridiculous that the library should be closed all day on Monday and every lunchtime!"[xxii]

The project team recognises that the current trend is towards better opening hours. It also recognises that there are considerable and recurring costs for library authorities in providing enhanced services. Nevertheless, it is firmly of the view that enhanced opening hours is the single best measure that can be taken in order to deliver a better service. This view is shared by librarians. A submission on behalf of two librarians says that "the biggest single barrier which restricts use of library services is perhaps the operation of opening hours which limit the ability of people to use library buildings"[xxiii]

The project team notes also that better service availability goes beyond the library service. All public services should be available to their customers at a time that suits the customer. With changes in work patterns and life-styles, this will mean increased week-end and late night opening of all public services.

As one of the most accessible public services, the project team believes that the library service should be in the vanguard when it comes to implementing this approach.

The project team underlines the fact that better opening hours does not always mean longer opening hours. The overriding principle should be that the library is open when it best suits the public. This will generally include being open during lunchtime, in the evening and at week-ends.

Implementing better opening hours will call for greater flexibility from library staff and library management. The project team accepts that better opening hours must be balanced against the available staff resources.

In that regard and with an approach that seeks to maximise opening hours, library authorities should take account of the possibility of interchanging staff at certain grades with the wider local authority staffing pool. Account should also be taken of the possibility of utilising staff drawn from the community or from FAS, for certain tasks.

It is not possible to give a detailed estimate of the cost of implementing a programme of enhanced opening hours at this stage but it must be stated that that the running costs and staff costs of libraries would naturally increase as the level of service increases.

In order to make a preliminary estimate of the impact of enhanced opening hours, a survey of 21 libraries, of varying sizes, in Dun Laoghaire - Rathdown, Cavan, Tipperary and Leitrim was carried out. It compared the existing opening hours with an enhanced level of service, consistent with the size of the population. On average, it resulted in an increase of approximately 20% in opening hours.

A survey carried out by the City and County Librarians Group of the Library Association of Ireland in 1994 sought to establish target opening hours for branch libraries. The response to the survey covers 46 branches and indicates an overall increase in opening hours of 40%. A simple average of the two rates of increase suggests that an overall improvement in opening hours of 30% is a reasonable target. The project team accepts that this is a very crude and generalised approach. There are many local circumstances in each library authority that will inform the scale and schedule of increased opening hours. Nevertheless, an overall increase of 30% is considered by the project team to be a suitable target for Library Authorities to aim for.

Translating increased opening hours into increased costs is also difficult to do. The 1998 estimates for the library service show that the operation and maintenance of the service accounts for £28.4 million out of a total allocation of £37.2 million. There is no information available on the proportion of the £28.4 million which is required to operate the branch network. However, the project team estimates that the figure could be as high as 65%.

A 30% increase in opening hours would then imply that the operation and maintenance element of library estimates would increase by 19.5%. (65% of 30%). In financial terms, this translates into an estimated cost for operation and maintenance of £33.9 million (existing + 19.5%). The project team accepts that this increase, amounting to £5.5 million per annum, will be phased in its introduction and that it represents, at current costs, the level of increase that would obtain in 2002.

The project team believes that with the need to boost the library service "across the board", library authorities and the Department of the Environment and Local Government should work together to address deficiencies in terms of service and infrastructure. In that regard, the project team supports the view that there should be a linkage between efforts to improve service provision and the level of capital investment.

"the project team supports the view that there should be a linkage between efforts to improve service provision and the level of capital investment"

Recommendations:

The project team recommends that Library Authorities should immediately commence work on developing a programme of enhanced opening hours. These should begin to be implemented during 1999.

In particular, the project team recommends that libraries should develop greater flexibility in their opening hours.

The project team also recommends to the Minister that funding for capital projects should be linked to the local development measures for improving the service, such as better opening hours.

A proposed target is that by January 2002, each library serving more than 10,000 customers would, as a minimum, be open through lunchtime each day, would be open each Saturday and would be open until 8.30 p.m. on at least two nights each week. The project team also suggests that consideration be given to Sunday opening where local circumstances indicate it is appropriate

Similar targets should be developed in respect of libraries serving smaller populations. Given the wide divergence in populations served and the different levels of demand throughout the country, it is not possible for the project team to recommend a single solution for all smaller libraries.

Recommendations:

In order to move as quickly as possible, it is recommended that each library authority should immediately begin to assess the need for adjusting opening hours and to investigate ways in which it might be achieved.

Each library authority should also research the cost of implementing enhanced opening hours in their area. They should also commence a process of staff consultation and negotiation to ensure that agreement on better opening hours can be agreed as early as possible.

7.2.2 Investing in library staff

The project team is satisfied that significant improvements in the quality of library services are necessary. Given the high level of staff input to the service, this will be best achieved through a programme of investment in library staff through implementation of Staff Development Plans. The project team does not believe that the current staff development arrangements are satisfactory.

Staff in libraries comprises professional, para-professional and support staff. Each library service needs a well-defined staffing structure, with an appropriate mix of professional, para-professional and support staff to help the public in all areas of provision, and enable libraries to adapt and respond to the public's evolving needs. In addition to the 'public face' of the service - staff working directly with the public - they also need a range of staff with specialist functions to support the work of front line staff. As the range and complexity of library and information services evolves, the need for specialist skills is growing in parallel.

The satisfaction of user needs depends to a major extent on the motivation, flexibility, initiative, enthusiasm, creativity, memory, current awareness, flair and imagination of individual members of staff. It also depends on appropriate staff/public ratios.

Very often in the past and even to the present day, library staff have provided a reasonably good quality service in inadequate surroundings, compensating to a considerable degree through their own skills and commitment for the overall lack of development of the service. This situation will not suffice in the future, given the challenges the service faces in terms of ICT, marketing, and other demands.

The library service envisioned by this report needs, not only qualified and committed staff, but staff trained and motivated in a manner designed to ensure that it achieves its potential.

The project team believes that professional staff receive adequate education and training to carry out the job of librarian. However, with the diversification in the role of the public library, it may be worth-while examining the course content of professional library courses to ensure that all of the needs of public librarians are met.

A more significant issue arises in the area of continuous professional development. The world of the library is changing rapidly and the skills appropriate to be a librarian 10 years ago are no longer adequate. Yet, there is no structured approach for librarians, particularly senior and chief librarians to keep up with developments or to contribute to developments.

The project team recognises the significant efforts made by individual librarians to maintain and develop their level of skills. The project team also recognises the efforts of the Library Association of Ireland in this regard. However, it is felt that a more systematic and programmed approach is necessary that would ensure that library authorities invest in the skills and talents of library professionals and get an appropriate return through service development and innovation.

"personnel must be adequately trained to use the equipment so that they can provide assistance to customers and also preserve the integrity of the medium"

In terms of para-professional staff, the project team believes that their contribution to delivering a better library service offers immense potential. It is para-professional staff who have most contact with the public. In smaller libraries, it is usually a para-professional member of staff who is the face of the library service and, for many people, is the librarian. The hard work and dedication of all library staff is acknowledged time and again in submissions to the project team. However, certain deficiencies are identified, particularly in the area of information technology. One such submission dealing with the library's role in life-long learning expressed the view that 'personnel must be adequately trained to use the equipment so that they can provide assistance to customers and also preserve the integrity of the medium'[xxiv].

While the arrangements for training and education vary from place to place, it is clear that many para-professional staff receive only basic training and that is mainly delivered "on-the-job". In circumstances where the approach of the staff is critical to the delivery of the service and where para-professional staff may operate largely unsupervised, it is critical that they are properly trained.

The project team acknowledges the difficulties faced by management in releasing staff for training, particularly in smaller service-points which may have only one or two persons serving. Nevertheless, the project team believes that a basic level of training should be professionally delivered which embraces dealing with customers, using information resources and ICT skills. Any minor and short-term disruption to the level of service delivered to the public will be more than compensated by the results of an effective staff development programme.

A structured training programme should also be open to all para-professional library staff seeking to develop their training and education within the library service.

The diversification of library services and activities poses new challenges for library staff. The project team believes that each library authority needs to look at the level of expertise that exists within its service in subjects outside the core area of librarianship. This includes such subjects as specialist ICT skills, group animation/facilitation skills, marketing skills, arts administration skills and heritage management skills. In addition, all staff should receive training on dealing with people visiting a library for the first time. (See section on improving access at 7.2.3 below)

Where skills exist within the service, arrangements should be put in place to exploit and develop them as far as possible. Where they do not exist, steps should be taken to acquire them. This might be through buying in training, recruiting specialists or through a consultancy arrangement.

The implementation of a proper staff development programme for library staff will help develop a

staffing flexibility which will allow greater mobility between the library service and other local authority services. It will also allow the deployment of staff, particularly at lower grades, sourced through FAS or the local community.

There is also a role for library staff in training other members of the local authority staff in particular subjects. As information-skills become an increasingly important part of administration and as One-Stop Shops develop, the need for local authority staff to confidently handle information and deal with the public will become vital. This is an area where library staff already have experience and expertise. This should be applied to the benefit of the local authority through library participation in designing and administering in-house training courses.

Recommendations:

Library authorities should recognise the long term commitment of their staff in a concrete way and devote the investment in human resources needed to take the library service into the new century.

The project team recommends that each library authority should formulate a Staff Development Plan. It is recommended that the plan should initially cover a 3-year period. The local authority Training Officer should be involved at each stage of the Staff Development Plan.

The project team recommends that An Chomhairle Leabharlanna should assist in the design of Staff Development Plans in a three way partnership that also includes the local authority Training Officer.

Formulating the Library Staff Development Plan
The Staff Development Plan should reflect the needs and scale of requirements to be put in place in order that the local authority can provide the services outlined in its overall library development programme. As one of the first steps in formulating a Staff

Development Plan for the library authority, the City or County Librarian in each library authority should undertake a training needs analysis.

The focus of the Staff Development Plan should be on the library service as a learning organisation with the chief librarian taking the responsibility for the continuing development of all staff under his or her direction. Part of the learning process would involve experimentation with new techniques.

The plan would outline formal courses, workshops, seminars, on the job learning, rotation of special assignments, projects and mentoring and other approaches such as exchanges, visits, conferences and meetings as appropriate for optimising staff resources.

"the project team supports the view that there should be a linkage between efforts to improve service provision and the level of capital investment"

The project team supports the view that there should be a linkage between efforts to improve service provision and the level of capital investment.

An Chomhairle Leabharlanna should also monitor, on a national level, feedback on the approaches taken by different library authorities, their contents and format and should liaise with library authorities on refinements to the plan.

The partnership between the County or City Librarian, An Chomhairle Leabharlanna and the local authority Training Officer should put in place a continuing system of staff development which is in line with the government policy in upskilling the public service.

The project team suggests the following stages for creating an effective Staff Development Plan:

- Outline the objectives of the local authority Staff Development Plan. Assess the training and development requirements from the local authority

library development plan and the appropriate objectives set.

- Discern the training requirements for working effectively in the library authority taking into account the functions as outlined in the Local Government Act, 1994.

- Consider the existing qualities and training needs of all staff.

- Design a Staff Development Plan, which will facilitate the development of skills required by the library authority and develop the knowledge base of all staff.

- Outline the required training and development methods for individuals, grades and teams.

- Assign a senior member of staff to implement the plan in full.

- Implement the plan, monitor and evaluate its progress and receive feedback from participants.

- Refine the Staff Development Plan in the light of this monitoring and evaluation and include the required changes in line with the changing environment in which the library authority operates. Full account should be taken of changes in the local authority's strategies and how they affect the development of library services.

This approach allows for adherence to the Staff Development Plan while accommodating the management of change.

Appropriate agencies such as the Library Association of Ireland, the Local Government Computer Services Board, Enterprise Ireland (formerly Forbairt), the Department of Library and Information Studies, UCD and the Institute of Public Administration should be considered for inclusion on the delivery of Staff Development measures. Other solutions will be addressed to assist in meeting specific requirements of library staff in the plan.

Open-learning for library staff

One such solution is the implementation of open learning for library staff. With the development of open learning programmes, it is now possible to provide a growing range of learning tools directly using ICT to the workplace. The project team believes that this can be particularly helpful for library staff as it allows flexibility in pursuing courses at the staff member's own pace and takes account of the demands of the library service. This approach may be particularly useful in branches with few members of staff and where it may be difficult to release staff for formal training courses without disrupting service to the public.

Recommendation:

The project team recommends that An Chomhairle Leabharlanna, in liaison with the local authority training officers and library staff, should assess how open learning tools can be optimised for library staff.

General Local Authority Staff Development Initiatives

It is important that the library staff are fully integrated in the ethos of the local authority. In particular with the evolution of local government and the enhancement of local services, it is likely that library staff will be in a position to form part of the local authority service provision.

Accordingly, it is vital that library staff participate in the general staff development programme for the local authority which will allow library staff to contribute to the training of other local authority staff in areas such as information management.

Recommendation:

The project team recommends that each local authority ensures that appropriate library staff are included in the general local authority Staff Development Plan and its programmes.

7.2.3. Improving equality of access to library services

The project team is satisfied that significant improvements in the accessibility of library services are necessary. Given the fact that the library service is intended for everybody in Ireland, a membership level of 24% and a usage level of 32% is unsatisfactory.[xxv]

The reasons for this are manifold and inter-related. However, the project team is satisfied that many people who would make use of the library are denied access to a satisfactory service. The project team is also satisfied that an enhanced service, as envisaged by this report, will go a long way to improving the take-up of the service.

Nevertheless there are some groups of people that are unlikely to use the library service until special measures are taken to facilitate them.

Recommendation:

In order to promote equality of access to the public library service, the project team recommends that each library authority should develop and implement a strategy to improve access to the library for everybody. The strategy should seek to overcome physical barriers to library use, social barriers to library use and financial barriers to library use.

The project team recommends that An Chomhairle Leabharlanna and other relevant organisations such as the Disability Support Service and the Combat Poverty Agency should assist in the development of access strategies and build upon best practise.

The project team foresees that the development of an access strategy will lead to improvements in providing access to the library for those who do not feel that the library is accessible for physical, social or any other reason. The strategy should also take into account general improvements being made to the service and build them in to the access strategy.

The strategy should be prepared and published by each library authority in 1999.

(a) Physical barriers

Among the chief groups who are denied access to library services are physically disabled people who often cannot physically get into library buildings and may also need special library materials or equipment; people with learning difficulties who need special training in using libraries and also special library materials and equipment and people in particular social circumstances (e.g. lone parents, shift-workers) who may need special arrangements, in order to facilitate their access to library services.

The importance of providing access to information and the role of libraries was identified in a number of submissions to the project team. This role was lucidly defined in a submission from the National Rehabilitation Board in these terms:

"Libraries have a fundamental role in providing access to information and, as such, need to ensure that users with disabilities have the same right to benefit from library services and are valued equally to other potential customers".

It is an issue which has been recognised by the Commission on the Status of People with Disabilities. It recommends that "Government should ensure that all libraries under the control of local authorities are accessible and carry a range of books in large print or talking books. Within 5 years, every public library should have an optical scanner."[xxvi]

The project team concurs with this recommendation.

The project team notes that since 1994 library authorities providing new branch libraries have been required to comply with Part M of the Building Regulations, 1991 (as amended by the Building Regulations, 1997). These provide that all buildings must provide access for people with disabilities.

The measures taken to comply with Part M usually apply to providing better access for mobility-impaired people through the provision of ramps, hand-rails and lifts.

Two issues remain to be resolved in this area: the upgrading of library buildings predating the introduction of Building Regulations and the suitability of library design, layout, stock and equipment to meet the needs of the disabled in ways not controlled by Building Regulations but which are covered by National Rehabilitation Board (NRB) recommendations and guidelines.

- As the Building Regulations are not retroactive, existing branch libraries have not been required to meet the standards set out in Part M. The Department of Environment and Local Government has requested local authorities to upgrade all their buildings, including libraries, so as to comply with Part M. However, the cost of doing so, while recognised as being substantial, has not been quantified in detail. As indicative costs, the provision of a wheelchair ramp costs approximately £5,000. The cost of a small lift would be in the order of £40,000.

- All libraries present difficulties for people with disabilities. For people with impaired mobility, circulation within a library can be difficult and access to certain parts of a library may be impossible. In addition, the shelving arrangements may militate against access to materials on either very low or very high shelves. People with these or other disabilities may not be able to operate library equipment such as PCs or microfilm readers. For people with impaired vision, access to many of the materials available in the library will be impossible. Likewise, people with reading or learning difficulties may not find adequate and up-to-date stock in the library. It is not possible to estimate the cost of improving library lay-out and equipment to meet fully the needs of people with disabilities.

One measure which has been identified is the provision of an optical scanner in each library. This is one of the recommendations of the Report of the Commission on the Status of People with Disabilities. The provision of an optical scanner ranges in cost from £1,600 to £4,500, depending on the functionality required.

Recommendations:

In order to improve access to library services for people with disabilities, the project team recommends that library authorities should include in their Access Strategy, measures to bring all of their libraries into compliance with Part M of the Building Regulations by 2006.

It is also recommended that compliance with NRB guidelines be implemented as far as possible in the same period and in consultation with the Department of Health and Children and its agencies such as Health Boards.

As regards services for the visually-impaired, the Access Strategy should include the provision of at least one optical scanner per 40 visually-impaired users. In 1989, there were 5,000 people registered as blind in Ireland. In general terms, this would suggest 125 scanners countrywide.

Snap Shot: *Innovative Services for Visually-Impaired Library Users*

The **TESTLAB** project, funded under the EU Telematics Programme, includes participating agencies from Ireland, The Netherlands, Austria, Germany, The U.K. and Italy. The project has established evaluation trials in a range of library sites aimed specifically at providing enhanced access to electronic documentation and to materials held in libraries through P.C. based communications technologies.

Co-ordinated in Ireland by the National Council for the Blind, trials have taken place in Dublin, Donegal, Tipperary and Fingal. The programme included the introduction of adaptive technologies, speech output devices and the integration of specialised braille and audio materials in a public library environment. A series of questionnaires responded to by visually impaired TESTLAB users in Dublin's Central Library, ILAC Centre, indicated significant levels of demand for services of this nature. Dublin Corporation now intends to continue the development and implementation of similar facilities, beyond the terms of the TESTLAB project, with a view to their future integration into normal public library provision.

Recommendation:

The project team recommends to the Minister that the Department of the Environment and Local Government should co-fund the provision of optical scanners at a rate of 50% in respect of 125 scanners over 3 years.

At an average cost of £3,000 each, there would be a cost of £375,000 over the period, shared between the Department and library a57uthorities.

Providing greater access is an issue that requires further research and the project team believes that the provision of greater access to people with disabilities is suitable for inclusion in the public library research programme outlined in Section 8 below.

"the project team recognises that the largest group of people who do not have access to a library are those who do not feel that they have access"

(b) Social Barriers
While physical barriers exclude a significant number of people from the library, the project team recognises that the largest group of people who do not have access to a library are those who do not feel that they have access. For them, there are very real social barriers to using a library. A survey carried out for Combat Poverty and the Arts Council[xxvii] shows that the library is more popular than any other arts or cultural institution amongst people living in disadvantaged areas. While this finding may offer some comfort, the same survey identified a number of barriers to participation in the arts that also apply to some extent to the library. These are: ticket price; overall cost (travel, child-minding costs etc.); a feeling that arts are for other people; nothing available locally; child-minding restrictions; a feeling that art is not

relevant to their lives; transport; previous unpleasant experience; lack of information; lack of time; lack of confidence and encouragement; sense of discrimination; lack of company.[xxviii]

The project team believes that public libraries have a very positive role to play in the lives of people excluded by these barriers. Access to information can offer a life-transforming opportunity to people living in poverty. Libraries are unique in the sense that they are theoretically available to everyone regardless of age, class, gender or political affiliation. As such they should be uniquely placed to influence the quality of life of those whom they serve.

The project team believes that giving people access to information should form part of the National Anti-Poverty Strategy. The project team believes that such access should be through the public library service and that the library service should be resourced to fulfil this role.

The submission to the project team from Combat Poverty states: "tackling poverty is about much more than ensuring that everyone has access to an adequate income. Combating poverty also means challenging the structures, institutions and public services, which reinforce and institutionalise social exclusion and inequality."

Recommendation:

The project team recommends to the Minister that there should be a national commitment to information access through public libraries. This should link to issues relating to information technology access, public information and freedom of information. It might take the form of a charter whereby the State guarantees that every citizen should be able to access all information at, or through, the local public library.

In terms of delivering access and overcoming barriers, the project team believes strongly that it can only be achieved by actively pursuing a deliberate strategy at local level that identifies the local barriers and removes them. Such a strategy will involve greater and better use of service points other than branch libraries and will require greater co-operation with other services such as health services, social services and prison services. Service-points in places such as community centres, hospitals and prisons, that are properly linked to the library service will give more access to more people than reliance on the branch network.

Some of the measures necessary to remove the barriers will be addressed by making the library service generally more available, by providing enhanced stock and by making proper use of marketing techniques. However, in order to overcome some of the less tangible barriers ("libraries are for other people", "not relevant to our lives", lack of confidence and encouragement etc.,) a more individual approach may be needed.

Recommendation:

It is recommended that the Access Strategy for each library authority should ensure that all community centres, community groups, community workers, adult education centres, adult education workers, home-school liaison officers, agricultural advisers, prison officers, probation officers and social workers be made fully aware of what the library has to offer. The mechanisms for achieving this will best be designed locally but may include such initiatives as "Open Days" for these services and regular briefings on library developments.

It is recommended that each library should have a named and trained person to act as a liaison with potential users who may be referred to the library by any other agency and that all library staff receive training on dealing with people visiting a library for the first time.

As a public service that sees itself as being for everybody, the project team believes that this issue will be the acid test for the continuing relevance of public libraries. Success in tackling this issue will make an enormous contribution to peoples lives and to the community. It will also reflect well on public libraries and increase their worth in the community.

"In preparing the Access Strategy, it is proposed that library authorities should consult with the local community and that the resulting strategy be published"

In preparing the Access Strategy, it is proposed that library authorities should consult with the local community and that the resulting strategy be published.

(c)   Financial barriers

The structure and scale of membership charges is cited as a barrier to library use, although the project team note that the issue did not arise to a significant degree amongst the submissions from the public. The project team is aware nevertheless that the Library Association of Ireland is opposed to any membership charges. The LAI concludes that until the Minister for the Environment and Local Government decides that the library service should be a free service, each local authority will continue to try to subsidise the service by charging for it.

The project team believes that library membership charges are a blunt instrument that in their present structure are inequitable. It also believes that they are only ever going to make up a small proportion of the cost of running the library service. Nevertheless, they represent some contribution from the community towards delivering a public service. In addition, the presence of a membership charge and the existence of a system of fines for overdue or damaged books can lead to a greater appreciation for some people of the value of the library service.

However, the project team notes that in many smaller branches, the amount of administration associated with collecting and accounting for charges outweighs the financial benefits to the library authority.

The project team agrees that membership or other charges must not be a barrier to library usage. However, it has decided not to make a general recommendation on the question of whether existing library charges should or should not exist. Rather, the project team believes that the issue is one that should be reviewed critically by each library authority.

"The project team agrees that membership or other charges must not be a barrier to library usage"

Recommendation:

The project team recommends that a review of library charges should be undertaken by each library authority during 1999. This review should focus on:

- **the structure of charges**
- **the scale of charges**
- **the cost of administering charges**
- **the level of service provided in respect of charges**
- **the equity of membership charges taking into account people's ability to pay.**

7.2.4 Improving specialised services

It is common practice at international level that large library systems offer specific subject interest or specific category services dealing for example, with education, genealogical research, music, art, community information or business. Even in small library systems, specialist collections, for example, local studies collections, are commonly available. Specialised services vary and may arise from specific community, environmental and social considerations or local industrial or business focus. These services are based on specialised collections of print and non-print materials facilitated by economies of scale and/or scope to provide a concentration of resources at one access point. They generally offer access to electronic resource materials and are exploited for public access and usage by librarians who have developed in-depth knowledge of the subjects and resource materials involved.

The project team recognises that such specialised services are core services, central to the role played by the public library in carrying out its objectives to identify and meet, the information needs of citizens of all ages, educational and social levels or sectoral

"it is desirable that specialised services relevant to local, regional, national or global communities should be developed"

interests. The project team believes that it is desirable that specialised services relevant to local, regional, national or global communities should be developed with materials made accessible directly to the public at local, regional and national levels as far as is feasible, with the assistance and mediation of professional expertise as necessary.

The project team is satisfied that in order to achieve this, significant improvements in the delivery of **specialised library services** are necessary. Given the high cost associated with providing such services, library authorities should take a pragmatic approach and deliver its range of services in a cost-effective manner.

The project team accepts that specialised services may not be available at all libraries. Where services are not immediately available, the project team believes that arrangements should be in place to give the best possible access to the service in a manner that suits the public.

The project team does not believe that library services should be exclusively mainstream, nor that services should be defined on the basis of crude value-for-money criteria. However the project team does believe that library authorities should understand, measure and/or describe the real and potential benefits of each service it provides. It should also measure its cost in terms of money, time, staff, accommodation and other resources, consistent with the social audit of the community.

The project team acknowledges that this is a complex area and that it is one where value judgements come into play - particularly in relation to benefits.

The project team believes that enhanced access to specialised services, materials and expertise, may be afforded by co-operative measures involving:

General development of a national networking capability designed to enable access at local levels to all collections, including specialised collections. (See Infrastructure at 7.3.)

The development of an inventory of specialised collections held in each library system to be made available via the world-wide web.

Production of bibliographic and other databases on specialist collections held at each library system, the database and index to be made available electronically for public access.

Development of regionally based Tele-Reference Centres, operated by library authorities, affording quick response to information enquiries including referral to government and other organisations as necessary, the Centres to be adequately resourced and serviced by qualified and appropriately trained staff .

The digitisation of non-print materials such as maps, prints, photographs for ease of public access in library buildings and for wider distribution in published format such as multi-medial CD-Roms and via the world-wide web.

Further research on the practicality of these measures will require further research and the project team believes that these areas are suitable for inclusion in the public library research programme outlined in Section 7.10.

Recommendations:

The project team recommends that library authorities, actively seek to develop their specialised services. Where appropriate, this should be in co-operation with other organisations and agencies who would benefit from the enhanced service.

The project team also recommends that some pilot or innovative measures, taken by library

authorities should be co-financed by central government sources where the outcome of the measure can be of benefit to other library authorities. Such measures should arise from proposals made through An Chomhairle Leabharlanna and approved and recommended for support by them.

Snap Shot: *Local Studies in Kerry*

County Kerry has a rich tradition in the areas of archaeology, history and antiquities. This is reflected in the recognition given to local studies within the Kerry County Library Service.

A comprehensive collection of books, tapes, prints and audio visual material has been built up over the years and is being added to on a regular basis. Where possible, microfilms of materials held only in national repositories have been acquired.

The Local Studies Section is located in the County Library Headquarters in Tralee. At present seating is available for 30 people. Facilities will be expanded in 1999 to allow a much wider range of services, i.e.

- increased space and seating;
- integration of archive material with local history;
- public access to a much broader collection of materials;
- facilities for lectures, exhibitions, etc.

The Local Studies Section is open to the public from 10.30a.m. to 5.00p.m. Monday-Saturday. Inquiries typically involve consulting a variety of sources which are all filtered through the librarian on duty. Telephone and postal enquiries from outside the county form a substantial part of the daily business.

The County Library has a purpose built archive unit which contains a comprehensive collection of archives material. In particular, the library holds the Minute Books of the Board of Guardians, R.D.C., Minutes and Board of Health Minute Books. At present the library does not have an archivist and some of the records remain uncatalogued.

The Kerry Archaeological and Historical Society, with a membership of 500, operates from the County Library. It produces a Journal and Magazine and provides an important link with local societies and events. The Society is closely integrated with the Local Studies Section to their mutual benefit.

The main categories of user of the Local Studies Section are:

- **Students**

The most notable increase in local history usage has been by students, primary, post-primary and third level. Changes in the school curriculum has led to an increased emphasis on local studies. Third level institutions are directing students to the County Library and the archival records are in very heavy demand.

- **Local Historians**

Local historians use the library on a continuous basis. Feedback on the facilities is invariably positive. In particular, they are pleased the County Library holds such a large collection thus avoiding the necessity on their part of travelling to Dublin.

- **General Public**

Increasingly, the general public are becoming aware of the local studies area as centre of both information and recreation. Newspapers, both local and national are most often consulted.

- **Researchers/Genealogists**

Genealogical research is a major reason for local history usage. Because Kerry was a county of high emigration in the 19th Century many Americans in particular return to find their roots. Many visitors allocate part of their holidays to genealogical research and some spend up to a week at a time in the local studies area. The County Library works in co-operation with the Killarney Genealogical Centre.

7.2.5 Improving libraries information services

The project team is satisfied that greater use can be made of library services to deliver information. The project team also believes that the library service can form an important interface with government at both local and national levels. The library can also be a valuable information service for Local Authority staff and local authority members. The project team believes that library authorities must be pro-active in developing the role of the library as information suppliers.

"the library network should be the primary source and should be a "First-Stop Shop" for information"

For a member of the public, seeking local information, the library network should be the primary source and should be a "First-Stop Shop" for information such as local geography, local history, local topography, local environment and local heritage. The library should also be a source for community information holding material on local services, local organisations, local enterprise, local tourism and local events.

The project team believes that such information should be presented in a manner that is easily accessible by the public. It should be actively kept up to date. It should include information in all formats from handbills to CD-Roms as well as more interactive formats such as websites of particular local interest.

As regards local authority services, the project team sees the potential of the library network for improving access to a range of administrative services to the public, such as making planning applications, paying motor tax etc., that are currently centralised in one or two locations in the local authority area.

At national level too, the library also has a role. The Government has given a high priority to the need for Ireland to meet the challenges and avail of the opportunities presented by the Information Society. In its first report (December 1997) the Information Society Commission highlighted the important part which the Government itself must play in this, not only in creating the kind of environment in which the Information Society can flourish, but also by "showing the way" i.e. providing easily-accessed, citizen-centred services as a model for other sectors to follow.

There has already been significant progress in adapting the delivery of Government services to this new demand. For example, comprehensive information is now accessible on the websites of Government Departments and various initiatives on the use of information and communications technology for service delivery are being developed. These initiatives will lead over time to "electronic government" - each citizen will have electronic access to comprehensive information on all aspects of Government services, will be able to communicate readily with Departments by e-mail, and will be able to carry out most of his or her dealings electronically with Government Departments, such as submitting applications, filing statistical or tax returns etc.

"electronic government must be accessible to all citizens, and not confined to those who have access to the necessary technology in their own homes or workplaces."

The prospect of electronic government offers substantial potential benefits for both the Government and the citizen. Service delivery will be quicker, more convenient and less expensive on both sides. However, if these benefits are to be fully achieved, electronic government must be accessible to all citizens, and not confined to those who have access to the necessary technology in their own homes or workplaces. Such a restriction, apart from being inefficient, would clearly be very undesirable on equity grounds.

It is clear, therefore, that the move towards electronic government will have to be accompanied by the provision of locations throughout the country, at which citizens can access the computers of the various Government Departments and agencies, obtain whatever information they require and carry out the various dealings which would previously have required written correspondence or personal visits.

The project team believes that the public library service, accessible throughout the country, provides an the ideal vehicle for this service. This report includes strong arguments supporting the provision of Information and Communications Technology for public use in the development of library infrastructure. The same technology will provide the basis for the universal accessibility of electronic government. In comparison to any other access points which might be considered, the library service has the advantage of trained staff who are comfortable with information, are used to dealing with the public. Library staff are also used to categorising, verifying and assessing the quality of information. With the explosion in information, particularly information delivered electronically, the librarian's experience as a mediator of information will be particularly useful, both in assessing information for the user and in transferring information-handling skills to the user.

Recommendations:

The project team recommends that the public library service should be put at the heart of public delivery initiatives of electronic government. If Ireland is to move successfully towards electronic government that is equally accessible to all, it is essential that the necessary infrastructure is put in place through the public library system.

The project team recommends to local authorities that they maximise the use of public libraries in providing access to their services by the public, so that the library becomes a gateway to government at local level.

7.2.6 Developing life-long learning services

Change is synonymous with the modern society. On the cusp of the new millennium, the rapidity and radical nature of this change brings into sharp focus the necessity for the individual and society to prepare for changed life-styles, work practices and career movements.

Such change involves an evolutionary approach to learning as an activity which pervades every aspect of life and which continues throughout life.

Certainly, movements in education generally illustrate that learning is no longer confined to a particular period of life or to an educational institution. It is learner-centred, availed of according to individual need, to inclination and to opportunity. Learning may be availed of via distance-learning means, using traditional or Internet-based methodologies, or open-learning flexible methodologies. Life-long learning has been described in a submission to the project team as "the defining feature of higher education in the twenty-first century and beyond".[xxix]

"The Public Library is identified as a long established community-based open-learning centre which uniquely is open and freely available to citizens of all ages and educational levels"

The public library is identified as a long established community-based open-learning centre which uniquely is open and freely available to citizens of all ages and educational levels. By definition, much of what the library already does contributes to life-long learning.

In essence, the public library is uniquely placed as a community-based pillar of learning opportunity, which is capable of creating, nurturing and sustaining awareness of the value of learning and of providing mediated access to resources which assist the process of learning throughout life. It imposes no entry criteria for the use of its resources and requires no evidence of individual progress to enable life-long access to its resources.

The project team is of the opinion that the public library can be an effective agent of change in building a learning society. Increasingly, the use by public libraries of information technologies as an educational tool for use by the public enhances the role of the public library in supporting education and life-long learning opportunity for children and adults. This is particularly true for those who are unable to participate in formal education for reasons of disability, isolation or who wish to engage in learning activity in parallel to undertaking career or family obligations.

The growth of knowledge based enterprise and the general increased importance of knowledge in economic activity means that the public library, by providing access to knowledge through its general and specialist collections and through the mediating professional expertise of its staff, supports employment potential and business developments. The library service can therefore be seen to provide economic benefits to society and a positive contribution to social inclusion which is to the benefit of all citizens in the evolving society.

The public library, by reason of its national penetration, its unique co-operative arrangements which operates at local, national and global levels, is recognised to be a key player in underpinning the process of life-long-learning.

At the same time, the project team is satisfied that greater use can be made of library services to deliver life-long learning opportunities. The project team is convinced that libraries need to take a more active position in this area. The project team also believes that other educational institutions and the Department of Education and Science can make much greater use of the services that libraries offer in this area. In particular, the current role that public libraries play in supporting distance education needs to be recognised. Public libraries are widely-used by students pursuing distance education to access study materials, to use reference material and advice and also to use as a study venue.

The project team welcomes the commitment from the Department of Education and Science to publish a Green Paper concerning lifelong learning and believes that the public library service should actively participate in the debate it will generate.

Snap Shot: *Adult Education in South Dublin*

South Dublin County Library Service contributes to the personal development of its customers, wishing to further their education by providing them with specific skills and advice and / or boosting their self-confidence. The library often provides the first necessary step towards involvement with more formal learning structures, particularly for those who have been out of the work environment for some time. The library provides a neutral and supportive environment in which individuals can learn at their own pace, where they do not have to be frightened of making mistakes and where they can make an investment in their own future.

Both the Central Library in Tallaght and Clondalkin Branch Library provide self-learning facilities for adults. Facilities include computer-based learning as well as audio and video based language learning facilities.

The self learning and CD-ROM packages in Tallaght and Clondalkin record a 64% usage. Facilities for adults in the self-learning centre in Tallaght library consist of:

- 3 PCs designated for computer tutorials. These range from basic computer literacy (Getting to Know Your Computer; Computers at Work) to specific software packages (Teach Yourself Excel 5; Teach Yourself Ventura Publishing);

- 3 PCs (with printers) designated for word processing / spreadsheet / database applications;

- 1 multimedia workstation with a wide range of applications including:

General knowledge - Encyclopaedias e.g. Britannia, Encarta;
Business - Kompass 98;
Culture - Bookshelf, Cinemania, English Poetry Plus, MS Art Gallery, Music

Central 97;
    Current affairs - European Citizens
    Information, Facts about Ireland;
    Geography/environment - 3D Atlas, Encarta
    World Atlas, Microsoft Oceans,

Planet Earth;
    Languages - Learn Irish, Language Labs
    German;
    Leisure - GMC Chess, Key Home Gardener;
    Literacy - New Reading Disc.

Recommendations:

The project team recommends to the Minister that the Department of the Environment and Local Government should actively co-ordinate a public library response to the issues raised in the Green Paper concerning lifelong learning and should take a constructive approach to any new initiatives proposed.

Furthermore, the project team recommends that the Department of the Environment and Local Government and An Chomhairle Leabharlanna should have a formal relationship with the Department of Education and Science centred on arrangements for life-long learning.

This might take the form of participation in the already-proposed national council for lifelong learning. This relationship should be mirrored at local level with a formal relationship between each library authority and relevant educational structures such as Vocational Education Committees, Third Level Institutions and the National Distance Education Centre.

Closer co-operation with the formal education system will ensure a more effective delivery of educational services and better exploitation of library resources. The project team recognises that substantial work needs to be carried out at local and national level to optimise the role of public libraries for life-long learning. Measures which should flow from

a new relationship between public libraries and the formal education system should provide greater support to learners. These include:

• **Developing facilitator training modules composed of:**

An educator awareness skills module which will enable librarians to deal more effectively with user enquiries.

Information technologies skills training which will enable librarians to fully exploit the possibility and potential of electronic information retrieval.

These modules should be included in the library Staff Development Plan outlined at 7.2.2.

• Equipping every public library with the necessary information and communications technologies which will enable access to the Internet and to other databases. (Infrastructure development is discussed in more detail at 7.3 below)

• Designating the public library system as a public access learning network.

• Developing strategic co-operative linkages with local, national and international educational institutions aimed at achieving learning infrastructure which is open and flexible and through which learning can be also delivered as necessary with the assistance of subject specialists.

• Developing databases and learning packages appropriate to the needs of defined community learner groups and individuals. Providing access to relevant learning packages / resources through public library Internet facilities.

• Developing and facilitating learning modules aimed at encouraging community learning programmes utilising library resource materials.

• Developing value added content packages appropriate to the needs of defined community learner groups and based on content held within local libraries.

- Developing a recognised certification of assisted
  learning effort carried out through the public
  learning access network, in association with
  strategically linked partners in the national learning grid.

7.2.7 Conclusion

This section has outlined the potential that the
library service has to offer in terms of providing
access to information, learning, knowledge and cultural services to every person in Ireland. The project
team believes that the measures outlined in this section can be achieved. The team is aware that the
effort and resources that will need to be employed at
national and local level will be significant in the context of the current provision for public libraries.
However the project team is also convinced that the
return in terms of economic development, social
inclusion and cultural development will be significant and will justify the investment made.

Notes

xxii   *Submission from Ms. Kitty Murphy, Cork.*

xxiii *Joint submission on behalf of the County Librarians of Fingal
       and South Dublin County Councils.*

xxiv   *Submission from the Open University Students Association*

xxv   *An Chomhairle Leabharlanna Statistics, 1995. IMS Omnibus
       Survey, 1997.*

xxvi   *A strategy for Equality, Report of the Commission on   the
       Status of People with Disabilities, 1996, Recommendation
       376, p 65.*

xxvii *Poverty: Access and Participation in the Arts, 1997,
       page 54.*

xxviii *ibid pages 82-85*

xxix   *Submission from the Open University Students Association.*

7.3.1 Current position:

All the measures for an enhanced service, outlined in the previous section, are dependent on an adequate infrastructural base being in place. It is clear to the project team that this base is not in place. A significant number of submissions referred to inadequate infrastructure with one person graphically describing conditions in his local library:

"the library is located on the second floor, accessible only by narrow stone steps. I had to negotiate a torrent of water which was coming from a broken downpipe. The steps were moss-grown and littered. The inside of the building was a shambles with the roof falling in and radiators falling off the walls"[xxx].

Infrastructure comprises:

- library buildings, including library headquarters;
- other service points such as schools, prisons, hospitals etc., not all of which is provided by library authorities;
- information and communication technology, including library systems, technology for public use and networks within and between libraries;
- mobile libraries and library delivery vans.

While there are approximately 320 libraries in operation in the country, the project team recognises that this **provision** is inadequate countrywide and that the provision is unevenly distributed. The project team is aware of some areas with populations of up to 30,000 people not having any library at all. Likewise, the project team is aware of long distances that some people have to travel in order to avail of a library service.

More significantly, the **quality** of the infrastructure in many places is sub-standard, being inadequate in size, poorly located, in a poor condition, poorly equipped or poorly stocked.

The main cause of this inadequacy is under-investment. The total capital investment by the Department of the Environment and Local Government in library infrastructure in the 20-year period 1978 - 1997 is slightly over £42 million.[xxxi] Of this, £16.3 million was invested in the period 1978-1987; and £25.8 million in the period 1988-1997. The allocation for 1998 stands at £2.76 million. In addition to this, library authorities also make some capital provision for their own library development. It can be seen that the 1998 allocation is slightly more than one-tenth of the total for the previous 10 year period. This implies that the allocation for public libraries has not kept pace with inflation to any significant degree. The allocation to public libraries has also lost out in relation to expanded capital investment by the Department of Environment and Local Government, particularly during the period of the current National Development Plan. Neither has it benefited from greater investment in arts which has taken place in recent years.

The relative investment in these other areas and the related cost of construction is set out in index form in the table below:[xxxii]

Year	Library Investment	Construction Prices	Department of Environment Vote	Arts Council Vote
1983	100	100	100	100
1985	66	113	124	115
1987	98	121	145	101
1989	86	132	97	144
1991	81	142	100	200
1993	131	148	120	237
1995	128	157	147	329
1997	114	165	162	421

This table, which shows the index for every second year, clearly shows that investment in libraries has fallen well behind other comparable sectors and lags behind increases in construction costs.

7.3.2 Need for infrastructure

The project team believes that everybody in Ireland has an equal right of access to information and learning. This access can only be delivered if a comprehensive network of library infrastructure is in place.

Access to information and learning is becoming more and more important. This is recognised by the Information Society Steering Committee which reported that "People are the most valuable resource to organisations in a knowledge-based economy because of their capacity to turn information into useful knowledge. The real potential of information and communications technologies, therefore, lies not in replacing people but in enhancing their abilities." [xxxiii]

"The project team believes that everybody in Ireland has an equal right of access to information and learning"

This situation is also recognised at European level where, for example, the first point made by the European Parliament Committee on Culture, Youth, Education and the Media in its own-initiative report on the role of libraries in the modern world is that : "the possession and mastery of information promote economic, social and cultural integration and therefore it is appropriate to organise and guarantee free access to information for the citizen." [xxxiv]

This sentiment is echoed in almost all reports and studies dealing with the information society and has been discussed in more detail in Chapter 4 of this report.

In practical terms, the library service assists in developing this society by:

- providing efficient and cost-effective access to new sources of information;
- acting as a support to business development in a knowledge-led environment;
- providing new skills and training opportunities to people to improve their participation in society as part of an anti-poverty strategy;
- providing a source of continuity during social and demographic change;

The project team believes that greater access to public libraries will enable more people to contribute to economic development through high-quality, information-based industry and enterprise.

As well as the economic benefits accruing from communities that have access to information through an enhanced library service and who possess enhanced information and ICT skills, there is a social dividend also. Libraries are institutions of personal development. The right combination of infrastructure, service and educational support will allow many more people participate in society.

A comprehensive library network with modern ICT infrastructure will also facilitate government in the better, quicker and cheaper delivery of those services which can be delivered electronically.

The project team believes that the existing level of infrastructure does not enable the acknowledged right to information and learning to be exercised equitably.

Providing equitable access to services is a difficulty that exists in relation to all public services in Ireland. The distribution of population throughout the country poses particular difficulties in delivering services to rural areas and to smaller urban areas in a cost-effective manner. However, failure to deliver adequate services contributes to a feeling of isolation in those areas, stymies development and makes them less attractive places to live. A similar situation, ironically, exists in some pockets of large urban settlements. Areas which are distinguished by high unemployment and poverty are frequently also denied high-quality services, which reinforces a sense of isolation and exclusion.

Accordingly, a tendency to provide infrastructure in those areas with larger populations must be countered by an appreciation of the need for a local development policy that is sustainable. £1 million invested in libraries in Dublin will obviously have an impact on a greater number of people than a similar investment in Co. Leitrim. Yet, that argument must be balanced by the need to invest in rural areas in order to develop their sustainability, to ensure their populations are maintained and to lessen the pressure on urban areas. This issue is discussed in more detail in section 7.4.

The project team believes that the development of modern library infrastructure, including advanced information and communication technologies can allow greater equity of access to information to all our citizens and be a powerful tool for social inclusion. When decisions on investment in infrastructure and services are being made, the project team believes that equity of access be a key consideration.

"the development of modern library infrastructure can allow greater equity of access to information and be a powerful tool for social inclusion"

Recommendations:

The project team recommends to the Minister that the public library infrastructure and services be developed to form a key component of a society that appreciates and understands the value of information, knowledge and learning. The library service should therefore be an important participant in Government initiatives to develop what is known as an Information Society.

The project team recommends to the Minister that the investment in library infrastructure and services should enhance equity of access to information and that it should form part of the Government's National Anti-Poverty Strategy.

Given the existing provision of library services and the benefits that are potentially available, the project team is convinced that greater investment in library infrastructure is justified.

"The best estimate that the project team can make is that the necessary infrastructure will cost over £90 million at 1998 prices"

The project team believes that a programme of capital investment, coupled with enhanced services will yield very positive results. The project team believes that such investment, properly managed, will be very good value for money.

The project team is not in a position to place a definitive cost on the investment required to provide the optimum level of infrastructure. It will be clearly a significant increase on the current level. The best estimate that the project team can make is that the necessary infrastructure will cost over £90 million at 1998 prices.

This estimate has been determined by the project team, having regard to:

- existing proposals for capital funding that are with the Department;
- the results of a survey on library infrastructure needs carried out by An Chomhairle Leabharlanna in 1993 (and updated for this policy review);
- library development programmes of library authorities;
- Public Libraries 2000 - A Programme for Development, published by the Library Association of Ireland in 1995;

The remainder of this section considers how the provision of library infrastructure and the provision of ICT facilities might be implemented. Measures dealing with enhancing the quality of stock are considered later in the report at 7.5 and those aimed at improving service provision have been discussed earlier in this report at 7.2.

Recommendation:

The project team recommends to the Minister that in order to position the public library service as a key component of the Information Society and to form an effective part of the National Anti-Poverty Strategy, a revised programme for investment in library infrastructure and services be put in place. The revised programme would address all the issues necessary to provide a library service that is available, accessible, comprehensive and of a high quality.

7.3.3 Scope and scale of revised investment programme

It is proposed that the revised programme would take a broader approach to library development than the current project-based scheme. It would embrace investment in infrastructure (including ICT infrastructure), in training, in services and in stock. The cost of the investment would be shared between the Department of the Environment and Local Government, library authorities and relevant third parties.

The programme should be implemented over an 8-year period, divided into two phases - Phase 1 covering 1999 to 2002 and Phase 2 covering 2003 to 2006.

The programme should address four key areas:

• Library infrastructure provision
• ICT provision
• Improvements in the range and quality of stock
• Improvement of Service Provision (length and scheduling of opening hours, staffing etc.)

The overall capital cost of the programme is estimated to be £93.5 million over 8 years. This is comprised of £75 million for library buildings and £18.5 million for ICT.

The project team believes that this is a modest sum when set against the benefits and when compared to investment in similar infrastructure in recent times.

Chapter 5 of this report outlines the current funding arrangements for library infrastructure. The project team believes that the situation whereby the Department provides almost 100% grant-aid for library infrastructure should be changed. A lower rate of grant would enable Exchequer funds to achieve more and would also reflect the improving financial position of local authorities. Circumstances where the library authority is clearly seen to be making a contribution to a capital project also has the effect of showing the commitment that it has to developing the range and quality of its service and enhances the sense of partnership between all the stakeholders.

The project team also believes that different rates of grant-aid might obtain in different regions but that a national ceiling of 75% should apply in respect of any investment. Furthermore, over the medium-term, the project team believes that the rate of grant-aid generally available would decline.

The nature and the number of submissions received by the project team has shown the widespread support that the public library has with the public. In some areas this has evolved into action groups such as Friends of Tipperary Library or ad hoc groups which get involved in local library development for example in Urlingford, Co. Kilkenny and Oranmore, Co. Galway. The project team believes that this goodwill and support should be encouraged and should be harnessed to help provide a better library service and a better library infrastructure.

"the project team believes that tax incentives should be available nationally for individuals or organisations investing in library infrastructure"

While the encouragement of local participation in developing a better service is primarily a matter to be worked out locally, the project team believes that tax incentives should be available nationally for individuals or organisations investing in library infrastructure. Tax-breaks have been in place since 1984 in respect of gifts for education in the arts and were extended in 1996 to other arts and educational areas. The project team believes that similar tax relief should now be extended to the public library sector.

Taking the revised rate of Exchequer support into account and also making allowances for financial input from other sources, the project team estimates that **investment by the Exchequer of £55 million over the next 8 years** is the appropriate level of support necessary to implement the improvements in infrastructure that are required. With the current allocation averaging £3 million p.a., the extra investment is approximately £30 million over the 8-year period.

In terms of opportunity cost, investing an extra £30 million in library infrastructure is the equivalent of 400-450 local authority housing units, less than 7 kilometres of motorway or 6 sewage treatment plants each serving a population equivalent of 25,000.

Snap Shot: *Branch Library in Dundalk*

Dundalk library, part of the Dundalk cultural centre project, is located in an early 18th century distillery building in the centre of Dundalk. The building and the adjoining tobacco warehouse are located in an area designated under the Urban Renewal Incentives Scheme and identified as being important is the town in maintaining a tangible link with its industrial and architectural heritage. The library is now a major civic building and through the excellence of its design is a delightful example of the maximum use of light and space.

The library has a total floor area of 1,111 m2 with a branch library on the ground floor and a reference library and administrative offices on the first floor. This impressive building forms part of civic complex which also includes a 1,852 m² museum and interpretative centre based in a converted warehouse. The best features of the old distillery buildings have been retained and many of the original roof trusses and floor timbers were salvaged for re-use. Two

wings were added, forming an atrium at the rear of the building. The space between the library and museum has been landscaped and there are plans to use this area for street theatre and outdoor exhibitions. A car park has been provided and a new bridge built across the river to give access to the library site.

Library facilities include adult and children's lending libraries, extensive audio-visual aids, newspaper and periodicals reading area, reference and study places. The Reference Library contains an extensive Irish history section as well as a special local studies section. Online Public Access Catalogues are available throughout the library.

The project team makes the following recommendations in relation to the funding of infrastructure:

Recommendations:

The project team recommends to the Minister that at least £55 million should be provided directly by the Exchequer, in the period 1999 to 2006 for a revised programme of investment in library infrastructure. This comprises just under 60% of the funding necessary to provide a level of infrastructure which will allow equitable access to library services.

The project team recommends to the Minister that a cap on exchequer funding of individual projects should be set at 75% of the agreed cost of the project.

The project team recommends that the balance of funding should be provided by library authorities and where appropriate should be raised from other sources such as corporate sponsorship.

The project team recommends that the Minister for Finance should provide tax-relief in respect of donations made to library authorities from

individuals and organisations in respect of library development. The relief should be in line with that available for gifts for education in the arts.

7.3.4 Operation of investment programme

In implementing the revised programme, it is proposed that a development programme be implemented by each library authority which looks beyond infrastructure provision and which includes implementation of the other measures recommended in this report.

Such a development programme would meet the requirements of the Local Government Act (1994) which require that

"A library development programme shall include -

(a) an outline of the existing service;

(b) the development objectives and priorities for the library service;

(c) the measures taken or proposed to be taken to secure those objectives;

(d) the financial or other implications of the programme;

(e) such other matters as are considered necessary by the library authority or as the Minister may specify."[xxxv]

Most library authorities have already produced library development programmes and these can form the background to an agreement with the Department in relation to co-funding the investment required for their implementation.

Any agreement reached with the Department would be on a multi-annual basis. Agreement on funding for infrastructure or other projects would be related to other improvements, particularly in relation to existing services, being implemented and funded by the library authority.

Recommendation:

The project team recommends to the Minister that a multi-annual agreement be sought with each library authority which links investment in library infrastructure with enhanced delivery of library services by that authority.

The project team proposes the following model as being a suitable approach to ensuring that such investment in infrastructure will result in greater benefits to the public.

Step 1:   Existing projects
The project team believes that projects that are with the Department, and have already received approval to seek tenders, should be funded in line with the terms of the existing scheme.

Step 2:   Prepare and publish guidelines for all other projects
The project team suggests that within 9 months of this report, the Department should publish guidelines on investment in public library infrastructure for the period 2000-2005.

"the Department should publish guidelines on investment in public library infrastructure for the period 2000-2005"

The Department's guidelines should be based upon the findings and recommendations of this report and should address two fundamental policy issues:

• the need to establish a network of modern public libraries which would be genuinely nation-wide, providing equal access throughout the state, while being locally accountable and locally delivered; and

• the need to equip Irish public libraries to play a key role in implementing the Information Society at a local level.

The guidelines should state what the Department wishes to achieve through its investment, and take into account priority objectives, including:

- equality and equity of access: ensuring that there would be an equitable spread of modern library facilities in each library authority area, or in each part of a library authority area in the case of larger authorities;

- social inclusion and anti-poverty strategies: giving priority to projects in areas with higher than average unemployment and areas suffering from other social problems such as loss of population.

- optimising ICT development: giving priority to projects which use ICT in a manner that best promotes the potential of information, knowledge and learning for the general public.

- promotion of local cultural development in a manner that is open to all.

- development of co-operation with other local services that have similar social, ICT or cultural objectives as the library.

- implementation of service delivery in a cost-effective manner; this may result in innovative service-delivery methods being employed to reach members of the public living in areas of small population or are in other ways isolated from the mainstream delivery of services.

The guidelines should state that all submissions for funding would have to be in line with the published objectives.

Step 3:   Invite applications for investment
Either simultaneously with the publication of the guidelines or very soon after, the Department should invite applications for investment for the 3-year period, 2000-2002, including investment in (a) new buildings; (b) upgrading of existing buildings; (c) fitting out. The Department would state the total amount of funding which it expected to be available over the 3 year period. A detailed discussion of the project team's approach to the provision of ICT infrastructure is set out at 7.3.5.

The Department should give target dates for decisions on applications. Projects should be submitted as part of an overall programme of development that respects the library development programmes required by the Local Government Act (1994).

All applications should be assessed on the basis of the objectives of the library authority's development programme and the library authority should also propose measures that it intends to take in order to deliver a better service from both existing and proposed infrastructure.

"The Department's contribution, while channelled towards specific capital projects should be tied to the implementation of the overall development plan by the library authority"

The Department's contribution, while channelled towards specific capital projects should be tied to the implementation of the overall development plan by the library authority. It should be open to the Department to vary the level of funding available, depending on progress at local level.

The Department's contribution should be on the basis that the library authority would have to bring matching funding of a minimum level of 25%, to the plan. The Department's contribution may also take account of projects already underway and in receipt of funding.

*Step 4:   Make preliminary awards, subject to
            library authorities accepting the terms*
The Department, having assessed the applications in the context of its own guidelines and objectives, and the development programmes of the relevant library authorities, should make preliminary awards. In general the Department's response would be to the development programmes rather than individual projects. Preliminary awards could be in two forms:

Firstly an allocation to individual projects, covering up to 75% of the cost of construction, IT, fitting out, and 50% for stock; or secondly a funding package based on the total cost of a library authority's development programme, enabling the authority to bring additional funding to the package and complete a greater number of projects.

Allocations in respect of projects or programmes would be on a multi-annual basis with moneys being drawn down on an annual basis.

Target dates for the commencement and completion of projects would be set out. library authorities would be informed of the basis on which awards would be made - why certain projects would be funded and others not.

Step 5:   Implement investment programme, and monitor progress
Agreements would be concluded between the Department and library authorities regarding the drawing down of funds, completion of projects, staffing, opening hours, bookfunds and other service-development measures. Monitoring of the programme would be more than a financial or desk exercise, and would involve assessments of how well they meet the objectives of the programme. An assessment of the programmes effectiveness in meeting the objectives at national level would also be carried out.

"Agreements would be concluded between the Department and library authorities regarding the drawing down of funds, completion of projects, staffing, opening hours, bookfunds and other service-development measures"

Step 6:   Revised guidelines for phase 2
A revised investment programme would come into effect in 2003. This should take account of the experience of the first phase and should offer less funding from the Department with more funding coming from local authorities. In principle the programme should operate in the same way, with the Department setting out what it wishes to achieve through its investment, and library authorities making proposals in response.

7.3.5 Information and communications technology infrastructure

Urgency of Development
The project team believes that the development of high-quality information and communication technology infrastructure will be a vital component in constructing a dynamic and truly accessible library service. The power and versatility of ICT will underpin many of the measures being proposed in this report as being necessary to develop the library service. Coupled with this, the pace of development in ICT is such that the public library service needs to get to grips quickly with the provision of ICT or risk being tailed off by other services that would not have an ethos of universal access nor would not be in a position to supply the added value in terms of mediation that the public library does.

The project team sees the provision of modern, powerful Information and Communication Technology as an important step in unlocking the potential of the public library as a centre for information, recreation and learning. It is convinced that the provision of ICT infrastructure must happen rapidly and consequently recommends that a national approach be taken to achieving this. While this is at variance with the general approach to development being locally led, the project team is convinced that the urgency for ICT provision justifies the approach recommended below. Such an approach will allow significant local input into the design of the implementation programme and will also allow significant economies of scale to be achieved.

"the provision of modern, powerful Information and Communication Technology as an important step in unlocking the potential of the public library"

Snap Shot: *Internet and Dublin City Libraries*

Public libraries in Ireland as elsewhere exercise a key role as facilitators and enablers of access to the information required by all citizens so that they can participate fully in an information rich age.

The Internet, demonstrably effective in assisting the process of communicating information both globally and locally, is widely used as a communication's medium by developed public library systems all over the world. The Dublin Corporation public library system was, in 1996, the first Irish public library to develop a website. The site has been significantly effective in attracting a wide local and international audience.

Information on the site of primary interest relates to public lending and reference service point locations, opening hours and services . The site also contains information on European Union assisted research projects and on the broad range of cultural services provided by the Dublin Corporation Public Library system. This includes the City Archive, Dublin and Irish Local Studies Collections and Heritage programmes. Additionally the site offers a significant amount of information on the International IMPAC Dublin Literary Award.

Importantly also, the value of using the internet is demonstrated in the context of interlibrary co-operation in a situation where the Dublin Corporation Public Library system has been able to co-ordinate an unparalleled level of international co-operation to the benefit of all involved.

The value of using the internet for promotional purposes is also evident in the VIRTUAL TOUR of Dublin City through which locals and visitors to the city are guided towards places of cultural interest. The Dublin Corporation Public Library system is using the internet in an innovative way to increase opportunities of access to information and to create audiences in Dublin and internationally for cultural content. It proposes in 1998 to offer public access via the internet to the catalogue of its collections and to further develop interactive services in this year. The development of the Dublin World Wide Website is part of a strategic approach to eliminating exclusion and deprivation in the information society with internet access being provided freely through the Dublin public system for those who would otherwise not be enabled to avail of the opportunities in the global village of knowledge.

Scope of ICT Development

There are three main strands to Information and Communications Technology (ICT) in public libraries:

- using ICT for housekeeping functions - accessions; cataloguing; circulations; and providing accurate, up to date management information on the performance of the service;
- using ICT to go beyond bibliographic records and give access to information and knowledge in all its forms;
- using ICT to create a national network of public libraries.

24 library authorities have already installed ICT to operate their housekeeping systems, either partially or totally. Investment is needed to fund the remainder, i.e. those authorities which have not yet automated and the remaining service points of those only partially automated. In addition, all library authorities will in time be required to update and upgrade their systems.

As outlined in Chapter 5, 20 out of 32 library authorities provide PCs for public usage. However, these are unevenly distributed within the library authorities and vary widely in what they allow the user to do.

A programme of investment in ICT will not merely provide hardware, software, communications and training for library staff. It will deliver access to content. The huge resources of public libraries will be made much more accessible to the public through this investment. It is envisaged that ICT investment will provide:

- a library of electronic resources selected by librarians, including their own databases, featuring local studies materials - bibliographic data and digitised materials;
- a genuine national network, accessible equally throughout the country and further afield;
- direct links to evaluated websites;
- an automatic web-based inter library loans system;
- a means of promoting the Gaelic language, and Irish literary and cultural resources.

The provision of ICT will achieve this by:

- giving access to the human record in whatever form it might be stored, in electronic formats as well as printed materials and multi-media;
- giving access to all government services, local and national;
- giving nation-wide access to all public library catalogues;
- making local business and community information accessible on-line;
- using ICT to offer full text, images, sound etc.;
- providing electronic document delivery,
- providing access to networks and support for net-navigation and info-searching;
- providing workstations for the public to create their own content;
- providing open learning and training opportunities;
- creating interfaces between the internet and on-line catalogues.
- digitising local studies materials.

The creation of a national ICT network which links the resources of individual libraries to form one on-line national resource will help to create a genuinely national public library service. This can equalise access to information and learning throughout the state by providing universal access to the normal holdings of each library, the special collections of each library, bibliographical data of each library and

the staff skills and expertise of each library. It will also facilitate the introduction of such desirable measures as a national membership system which allows a person to use his or her local library membership to use the services of any other library authority.

"investment in ICT will be the thread that will bring together all the improvements being made in each library authority"

The project team believes that investment in ICT will be the thread that will bring together all the improvements being made in each library authority and will make them available to everybody in the country.

Recommendations:

The project team recommends that all public libraries should, as a matter of urgency, upgrade the level of ICT infrastructure and services they offer to the public.

Given the urgency of the need and the national scope of the programme, the project team recommends to the Minister, that a national approach be taken to ICT provision, which while centrally managed, would have a strong local authority input. The project team recommends that up to 75% of the cost of the investment should be available from the Exchequer

The proposed investment will cover:

- connectivity,
- hardware (new or upgraded),
- maintenance,
- training and up-skilling for staff
- training and tutoring for the public.

The first steps to be taken are to provide Internet access to the public through all public libraries and to complete the automation of housekeeping functions of libraries.

It is proposed that responsibility for designing and implementing a programme to achieve this lies with the Department of the Environment and Local Government, with support from An Chomhairle Leabharlanna, the Local Government Computer Services Board and the Information Society Commission. It should be implemented by the year 2000.

Recommendations:

It is recommended to the Minister that funding be put in place immediately to allow the investment programme to commence quickly. It is also recommended that the programme be phased, with Phase 1 starting immediately and providing Internet access in each of the larger libraries and commencing the training programme for library staff

Phase 1 would also include automation at headquarters and at branch level of those libraries not yet automated.

Phase 2 would target medium-size and smaller libraries for Internet provision and upgrade the automation of other library authorities.

It is assumed that each library will be stand-alone at first and will not be networked with other libraries within the local authority. However as local authority Wide Area Networks and Intranets develop, libraries should be included.

It is also recommended that a strong programme management structure be established. This will allow the development of ICT facilities to be carried out in a rapid and cost-effective manner. It will also allow the development of ICT infrastructure in a manner that is best suited to a library environment.

Issues to be addressed by the project management include:

- technical issues concerning the best ICT architecture and configuration;
- value-for-money issues concerning the procurement of ICT equipment and services;
- training issues for library staff, management and users;
- capacity issues concerning the introduction of significant new services into small and perhaps unsuitable library buildings;
- system management issues concerning the ongoing running and development of ICT services in each library authority.

7.3.6 Conclusion

It is clear to the team that a high quality library infrastructure and services have a positive contribution to make to Ireland's future. It is also clear that we are some way short of what is needed. The project team believes that investment in the areas outlined in this section will enable Ireland to have a secure platform of access to information, knowledge and learning that will be vital to continuing economic, social and cultural development.

Notes

xxx   *Submission from Mr. Patrick J. Waters, Donegal.*

xxxi *This analysis of is based upon summary figures in the Department for capital funding and for subsidy paid by An Chomhairle Leabharlanna. The analysis of library authority expenditure is based upon "Public Library Statistics 1988-1994", published by An Chomhairle Leabharlanna in 1996 and on "Public library authorities - Annual Estimates of Expenditure 1997"*

    Figures not adjusted for inflation.

xxxii *Sources: CSO, Volumes of Estimates, Appropriation Accounts*

xxxiii *Information Society Ireland, Strategy for Action, December 1996 p. 7*

xxxiv *Report on the Green Paper on the Role of Libraries in the Modern World; EP Committee on Culture, Youth, Education and the Media; Rapporteur: Mrs. Mirja Ryynnen; June 1998*

xxxv *Sections 33(5) and 33(6) of the Act.*

The previous section of this chapter dealing with infrastructure highlights the difficulties that exist in providing equitable access to public services in a country with a demographic distribution like Ireland. The 1996 Census of Population showed that 1,518,096 people live in the "Aggregate Rural Area", which is defined as areas outside population clusters of 1,500 or more inhabitants. A further 260,993 people live in towns with a population of fewer than 5,000. Accordingly, it can be said that 1,779,089 people or 49% of the population live in rural areas or in small towns.

Clearly, it is difficult to operate services in areas of small population in a cost-effective manner. This applies to all services. Cut-backs and closures in services like Post Offices, Garda Stations and ESB Offices have been evident in recent years. The project team is under no illusion that the library service can easily buck this trend and that it will be able to offer a traditional fixed-point service in a dedicated library building to all the population close to where they live. However, the project team believes that innovative approaches to service delivery can result in a high-quality service being equally available to everybody in Ireland.

In some areas of large urban developments, the sense of isolation from public services can be no less real. These areas are sometimes, but not always, distinguished by large-scale, poor-quality housing, high unemployment rates and widespread poverty. They are areas where public transport is often deficient and where car-ownership is low. In addition, social and family commitments often reduce mobility still further. In those circumstances, a visit to a library situated in the city-centre or town-centre is not easily-achieved. Residents in these areas are often as difficult to reach with library services as even the remotest parts of rural Ireland.

One element of service-delivery which will continue to be used in rural and urban areas is a fleet of mobile libraries. While mobile libraries are effective at reaching small populations and isolated communities, they are restricted in the range of material they can offer by the limitations in their capacity.

Likewise there are limits to the other library services that they can offer. Another disadvantage to mobile libraries is that they are expensive to run, with the average cost of issuing a book being about twice the cost of issuing a book from a branch library. They also need replacing a lot more frequently than library buildings.

"innovative approaches to service delivery can result in a high-quality service being equally available to everybody in Ireland"

Nevertheless, a well-designed and tailored mobile library service can succeed in delivering a high quality service to the most isolated parts of Ireland.

The project team believes that the integration of greater ICT within mobiles should be considered. Application of appropriate technology should allow users to receive the same ICT services as users in branch libraries. The project team also believes that mobile libraries can be used to deliver associated services, such as arts activities or information campaigns, to small communities. The mobile service has the advantage of being an established service and having a known customer-base which should allow services to be tailored to meet the needs of the community.

- The project team believes that mobile libraries can be only part of the solution, however, and that radical new approaches are needed if every potential library user is to be reached. It is clear that further research is needed. The project team believes that the following two approaches should be investigated and adopted where appropriate:

- Combining library services with other local services. For example, a local shop might be franchised to reserve a section for library material. This material, specially selected to match the local population profile, would be available when the shop is open. Material could also be ordered, which would be delivered to the shop. A spin-off benefit is that it may help generate extra activity in rural shops, some of whom find it difficult to compete with urban retailers.

- Where access to ICT is available in an area, either in the local school or community centre, access to the library service could be put in place whereby catalogues could be browsed, other library material could be accessed and orders could be placed. It may then prove cost-effective to deliver material to users directly, either by post or by other means.

Recommendations:

The project team recommends that library authorities should carry out a fundamental review of how it serves isolated communities, whether rural or urban. library authorities should be prepared to use innovative solutions to meet identified needs.

The project team recommends that An Chomhairle Leabharlanna should include research into innovative service-delivery methods in the programme of research to be carried out under its aegis. The research should look at international efforts to deal with this issue, particularly in countries similar to Ireland, for example, Scotland and Denmark.

The project team recommends that the Minister should make a small allocation available to pilot some innovative solutions in an Irish context. The sum available might be £100,000 over two years. The pilot projects might be carried out and co-funded in association with other government departments which are trying to tackle similar problems in respect of their services.

7.5.1 Library authority bookfunds

The project team is satisfied that significant improvements in the range and quality of stock in library services are necessary.

The project team acknowledges the increases that have generally been made by library authorities in recent years. However, it must be noted that these increases are on a very low base.

The project team also notes the wide diversity that exists in bookfunds between library authorities. With the cost of a book averaging £25[xxxvi], the project team is strongly of the view that a bookfund of less than £1.00 per head of population is unacceptable. Yet the project team notes that for 1998, two-thirds of library authorities allocated book-funds equivalent to £1.00 per head, or less.[xxxvii]

The project team believes that if library authorities are serious about delivering a proper service to its customers, it must make adequate material available to them. Experience has shown the link between stock and usage. Members of the public are not going to make use of a service that is old, static, worn and out of date. A large number of the submissions to the project team referred to the quality and quantity of stock in public libraries. One such submission states "I find the library very good for the 2-10 age group but after that the number of books in stock declines as does the quality. Teen reading largely comprises 'teen pulp' which, while good for a light read, is not great. The transition from children's to adult books is a big one and while the market is better served now by the many new Irish authors, the number is still relatively small" .[xxxviii]

"the public are not going to make use of a service that is old, static, worn and out of date"

The project team acknowledges that maintaining high quality stock is difficult. In particular it is noted that the diversity of stock formats places new demands on library authorities. In the past, stock was limited to books and periodicals. Now stock must embrace books, periodicals, specialised video tapes, compact discs, CD-Rom products and on-line services. In addition, the amount of material published in each format is continuously expanding. This is partly due to the dominance of the English language in publishing. In 1996, there were in excess of 100,000 titles published in the UK alone.[xxxix] By way of contrast there are fewer than 5,000 titles published in Portugal annually.

The expansion in higher education has had an impact in this area also. Increasingly, third-level and further education students are making use of public libraries to source material. This particularly applies to students availing of distance education. This, in turn, gives rise to demands for specialist material that may be of appeal to a limited number of people and can also be very expensive. This includes non-book material such as software licenses.

More generally, the dominance of UK publications means that most stock is priced in Sterling. This leaves library authorities exposed to fluctuations in exchange rates. For example, on 1 May 1998 Sterling had appreciated in value against the Punt by 17% since January 1997 and by 7% since October 1997 when local authority estimates were prepared.[xl] This translates directly into increased costs for stock. In an environment of limited resources, it means fewer stock purchases.

Recommendation:

The project team recommends to the Minister that he should work with library authorities on a programme to generally upgrade the stock of public libraries. In that regard, the project team notes that the impact of a special grant for bookstock made by the Minister in 1994 was instant, positive and enduring.

That grant of £2 million gave library authorities a jump-start in regard to stock quality. The trend since 1994 has generally been upward, with the 1997 total bookfund allocation being 135% of the 1994 figure allocated by library authorities. The 1998 allocation sees a further 10% increase.

However, the project team emphasises that it is primarily library authorities that must take action to improve the range and quality of stock in public libraries. The project team believes that a substantial increase in bookfunds nationally will be a key factor in improving the service delivered by public libraries. The project team also sees merit in an approach that would link improvements in bookfunds by library authorities to developments in other areas, notably investment in infrastructure.

Recommendation:

While recognising the general difficulties faced by library authorities, the project team strongly recommends that a programme of bookfund increases be undertaken by each library authority.

The project team also recommends that a national target should be agreed by all library authorities. It is proposed that the target would be that by 2002, each library authority would invest at least £2.50 per capita in bookstock annually.

Implementing this measure by 2002 will increase the level of investment from the 1998 level of £4.60m to an estimated £10m p.a. On average this is a 118% increase, but the range of increases is from 40% to 745%.

Recommendation:

In order to help library authorities achieve the necessary increase, the project team recommends to the Minister he should allocate a national book grant totalling £3.6 million over four years from 1999. This should be structured as follows: 1999: £1,000,000; 2000: £1,000,000; 2001: £800,000 and 2002: £800,000.

The funding should be distributed by An Chomhairle Leabharlanna according to a formula agreed with the Department and library authorities. The grant should be reviewed in the latter half of 2000 and adjusted if necessary for later years. The formula should be designed to reward library authorities showing most improvement in their bookfunds over an agreed period.

7.5.2 Primary school library bookfund

The project team acknowledges the funding provided by the Department of Education and Science for bookstock for primary school libraries. In particular, the project team recognises the significant increase in the level of support that took place in 1995 and 1996. The grant currently stands at £2.12 per pupil and totals £973,000. The project team supports the existing arrangement whereby the grant is paid to library authorities who then supply the books to the schools libraries. This enables the expertise of trained librarians to be applied to the selection of materials. The input of the library authority in providing the service surrounding book-selection, cataloguing and stock management should not be disregarded.

"the project team would like to see support offered to post-primary school libraries"

The project team believes that greater resources are still needed by schools libraries. In particular, the project team would like to see support offered to post-primary school libraries. The project team also recognises that support for schools library services go well beyond the funding of bookstock. These issues are discussed in section 7 of this chapter.

Recommendations:

The project team recommends to the Minister for Education and Science that the per capita increases for general bookfunds implemented by library authorities should be matched by increases in the per capita bookfund grant for primary school libraries made by the Department of Education and Science.
The project team also recommends that the Minister for Education and Science should con-

sider providing a specific bookfund grant in respect of post-primary schools where a school library is in operation. Where these libraries are operated by the library authority, the grant should be channelled through the library authority in the same way as the primary school grant.

A proposed target for primary school pupils is that the per pupil allocation would be increased to £3.00 by 2002. This target is slightly higher than the target for the general public because the project team believes that the savings to schools in meeting the cost of supplying staff which is met by library authorities should be put into greater bookfunds for pupils. Meeting the proposed target would result in an annual allocation of £1.377 million, based on the current number of primary school pupils.

7.5.3 Inter-library loans
The project team believes that greater co-operation between library authorities in relation to inter-lending is a worthwhile alternative to purchasing expensive stock. The team notes the existence of the Irish Joint Fiction Reserve Scheme which aims to hold out-of print fiction in a distributed fashion and to make it available to other libraries on request. The project team believes that a properly resourced Joint Fiction Reserve Scheme, coupled with nation-wide access to public library catalogues can form the basis for greater exploitation of existing bookstock and remove some of the pressure on library authorities to hold copies of material that may be available elsewhere.

Recommendation:

The project team is also aware of the difficulties that exist in relation to the existing scheme and recommend that the Committee on Library Co-operation (COLICO) examine the situation with a view to putting in place measures that will facilitate greater participation in the scheme by Irish library authorities.

Notes
xxxvi Source: 'The Bookseller', January 1997
xxxvii Source: Public library authorities, Annual Estimates of Expenditure 1998, An Chomhairle Leabharlanna
xxxviii Submission from Ms. Barbara Whelan, Dublin
xxxix Source: 'The Bookseller', January 1997
xl Source Central Bank

7.6.1   Promotion v marketing

The project team is satisfied that significant improvements in how libraries are promoted and marketed are necessary.

The project team recognises that marketing is a far easier issue to call for than it is to implement. With reference to the issue of delivering an enhanced service, discussed above, the project team believes that an essential prerequisite to any marketing strategy is that there is a service in place that is worth marketing.

"marketing is a far easier issue to call for than it is to implement"

Marketing goes well beyond promotion and advertising. It involves positioning library services in the mind of the public in a fashion that attracts its support. The topic has been discussed by Blathnaid McGeough of Tallaght RTC in Local Authority Times.[xli]   She cites a definition of marketing as "the management process responsible for identifying, anticipating and satisfying customer requirements profitably". The tools listed as being essential for marketing include:

*   market/client research,
*   development of services,
*   provision of services and
*   on-going monitoring of service quality to ensure client satisfaction.

The project team believes that these tools need to be applied at a national level and, more importantly at a local level.

Most library users will be local. Accordingly, the project team believes it is important that the service is marketed locally. This means that the library service must get to know the needs of the membership and more importantly, the needs of the potential membership. This must be done in a structured fashion. "Gut-feel" must be replaced by research.

The limitations of a "gut-feel" approach were exposed by "Turning Over a New Leaf"[xlii], a report by the General Consumer Council for Northern Ireland. It points up the differences in perception between librarians and library-users. A survey of 360 non-users suggested new services and facilities which would encourage more visits or more use of the libraries. The top 3 suggestions were:

*   Refreshment facilities\café (54%),
*   More evening opening (31%),
*   Wider range of books (28%).

The same survey asked 171 librarians to prioritise improvements they felt necessary in the service. This yielded a contrasting top 3 suggestions of:

*   More spent on books,
*   Better marketing\ publicity and
*   New services based on electronic media.

More evening opening was 6th in priority and refreshment facilities\café did not feature at all in the librarians' list of 10 measures.

7.6.1 Promotion of libraries at national level

The project team is aware of the numerous calls that have been made for a national campaign to market libraries. For example, a submission from a library authority recommends that: "A marketing strategy for public libraries, focused in particular at national level and possibly issues-driven, is required. This could be delivered through a Marketing and Press Service which could be associated with the Research Department of An Chomhairle Leabharlanna." [xliii] The project team, however, believes that any national marketing campaign must be built upon and grow from local marketing campaigns.

The project team believes that any promotional campaign, as distinct from marketing, carried out at national level, seeking to attract greater use of the library would not be very cost-effective. However, the project team believes that a national approach to promoting certain events such as Children's Book Festival, the children's essay competition run by An Chomhairle Leabharlanna or World Book Day would stand a better chance of being effective. Such a promotion would have to be linked to local activities which take place on a similar basis nationally.

The project team believes that a promotion campaign which promotes the public library as a **gateway to the information society** would be of benefit to the library. It also believes that such a campaign would also be of benefit to organisations charged with overseeing and steering Information Society developments in Ireland and the EU.

Recommendation:

The project team recommends that An Chomhairle Leabharlanna should work closely with the Information Society Commission to ensure that the public library service is an integral part of measures to develop awareness of the information society.

"library authorities must take a deliberate, dedicated and pro-active approach to local promotion"

7.6.2 Promotion of libraries at local level

More generally, the project team believes that the promotion of local library services is best carried out using the usual range of local media. The project team believes that library authorities must take a deliberate, dedicated and pro-active approach to local promotion, if it wants to succeed against the clamour of other activities and services available to the public. The investment of time and money should not be underestimated.

In that regard, many of the marketing and promotion issues that are of concern to the library will also be of concern to local authorities in general. The project team believes that libraries will benefit from a synergistic approach to promotion and marketing with the wider local authority. The library service must also be prepared to put some effort into marketing the library service <u>within</u> the local authority. library authorities should also be aware of the different needs of different categories of library-user.

Children's needs may be different to adults and the services offered in a rural area may need to be different to those in an urban area. These are issues that can be researched locally. However, information and communication technology now offers library authorities the possibility of promoting certain aspects of their service to a global audience.

The project team believes that libraries should pursue this aspect of their service. It believes that this should be done with care and should always bear the audience in mind. As far as possible the library should identify communities or groups of users who use the Internet to access library or other local services or might benefit from Internet-based services. This will not be as straightforward as with users who can be met face-to-face and new research techniques may need to be applied.

The library Internet presence should be tailored to meet the particular needs of Internet users. For example, while it is important for local library users to be aware of opening hours, it may not be so relevant to users who access the library through the Internet and who may be living in the US. On the other hand, links to other web-sites outside the library and perhaps outside the local area may be very useful to such users.

In order to optimise the use of the Internet as a marketing tool, the project team recommends that each library authority review its Internet presence to determine whether it best fits the needs of a category of user that may have different requirements to other users.

Recommendations:

In order to market library services effectively, the project team recommends that each library authority carry out a programme of research into what their users and the public in their area want from the library. The project team suggests that this may be done as part of a wider market-research project covering the entire local authority.
The project team also recommends that a local

marketing plan be developed by each library authority, based on the results of market research. This should be carried out during 1999 and should be published. While, this may be done as part of a local authority-wide marketing plan, the library service should be clearly identified within it.

7.6.3 Marketing of public libraries at national level

Marketing of public libraries at national level must by definition take a different approach. The project team believes that the marketing of libraries at this level should primarily be aimed at decision-makers in government and in other agencies that can help library authorities deliver a better service. For example, a successful marketing approach at this level will lead all information suppliers to include the public library network amongst its outlets. The library services that are available should be known to information suppliers and the functions of the library as: "a resource for Information and Learning, a resource for Culture and the Imagination and a resource for Children and Young People" should be understood by decision-makers.

Recommendations:

The project team recommends that An Chomhairle Leabharlanna accepts the role of marketing public libraries at national level. The project team clearly sees this role as being different to running national advertising campaigns or other promotional activities. It should focus on the contribution that the library can make to issues such as ICT awareness, literacy and lifelong learning.

The project team recommends that An Chomhairle Leabharlanna should establish a project with input from marketing consultants to advise on how public libraries can be best positioned nationally to influence decision-makers on the benefits of public libraries. The project should also provide advice to library authorities on how library services can be marketed locally.

A national marketing approach to decision-makers can be replicated at local level. The project team believes that involvement by library authorities with other organisations and institutions (such as schools enterprise and community groups) can be used to show the value of a dynamic library service to those bodies and their customers. This is discussed in more detail at 7.7.

Notes

xli   The role of Marketing in Public Sector Management, Local Authority Times, Spring 1996, pp 8-10

xlii   Public Libraries - Turning Over a new Leaf, General Consumer Council for Northern Ireland, 1995, 2 Vols

xliii Submission from Wexford County Council

7.7.1 General

The project team believes that the library exists, not for its own purposes, but as a service to its users. The service must meet the priorities of the users. In that regard the project team believes that the library service must be outward-looking and in touch with its user-base. This is achieved through interaction with its users and through marketing measures as outlined above. This approach will lead to demands for information services that the library cannot meet on its own. It necessitates co-operation with other libraries and information services and co-operation with organisations and groups that are neither libraries or information services.

While the project team recognises the policy of library authorities to co-operate with others, it also recognises that a more proactive approach needs to be taken in order to ensure that co-operation is as effective and as comprehensive as possible, not least in maximising the use of library resources.

"a more proactive approach needs to be taken in order to ensure that co-operation is as effective and as comprehensive as possible"

Recommendation:

Accordingly, the project team recommends to library authorities that they develop a library co-operation strategy. The strategy will develop an approach to resource sharing and better service provision that will embrace co-operation with other libraries and also with a wide range of groups and organisations operating locally.

The focus of the strategy should be to support the library in meeting the needs of the local community. The library co-operation strategy should be prepared by library personnel in each library authority area. It should relate to the wider engagement undertaken by the local authority with the community. The strategy should be prepared during 1999 and should be published.

In preparing the strategy, library authorities should consider convening a series of fora of service providers in the community to formulate a strategy to meet the library needs of all the local community.

Recommendation:

The project team recommends that a national focus should be placed on co-operation. Accordingly, the strategies for each library authority area should be incorporated into a national strategy which can be used to agree appropriate measures with all players at national and international level. The project team recommends that An Chomhairle Leabharlanna should oversee and facilitate this measure in association with local authorities, government departments, library and information providers, educational support agencies, arts bodies and other agencies, as appropriate.

Further research is required into all aspects of co-operation. The National Policy on Libraries and Information Services Project, due to report in Spring 1999, will provide recommendations for future strategic alliances between the different library sectors and with other agencies. In formulating a national strategy on co-operation for public libraries, account should be taken of its recommendations.

The three main strands in a library co-operation strategy will be the development of a national network of libraries through resource-sharing, co-operation with other local services and co-operation at EU and international level.

Snap Shot: *Books Across the Border*

Louth County Library and the Southern Education and Library Board have received funding under the Special Support Programme for Peace and Reconciliation to develop a project on the theme of parents, children and reading. The project "Books Across the Border" involves setting up a pilot scheme in Dundalk and Newry to offer parents support and guidance in relation to children's literature and reading.

One aspect of the project is a series of seminars to be held over 5 weeks at Dundalk and Newry Libraries. Speakers at the seminars include Joan Linqard, Tom McCaughren, Marilyn Taylor, Robert Dunbar, Dr. Tony Humphreys, Peter Regan and John Quinn.

In addition, students on both sides of the border are currently reading and reviewing the literature on the troubles which has been specifically aimed at teenagers. I.E.S. Ltd., have kindly donated a "Peace Collection" of titles which reflect this theme. The collections will be available for block loan to schools in the Dundalk and Newry areas in due course. Tom McCaughren's 'Rainbows of the Moon' has been selected as the project's "theme" book and copies are being distributed accordingly.

As the project has been very well supported the libraries have applied for funding to extend the project into 1999 and 2000. An application for phase 2 funding has been made which would allow the library services to develop the project into the area of historical fiction and reminiscence work for adults. The concentration in Phase 2 on border lives and shared memories, which reflect cross border experiences, will form the basis of training for adults in creative writing - linking with children's exploration of this fiction through competitions and workshops.

Co-operation on this project has provided a structure for further co-operative projects between the libraries. The areas of children's services and heritage are viewed as the areas with most potential for development.

7.7.2 Development of a national network of libraries through resource-sharing

The project team understands that the simple act of providing library material masks a complex set of processes. However, library-users are blind to these processes. Whether the item they want is on the shelf, has to be ordered or is available on-line is largely irrelevant. The user's abiding interest is in satisfying their need for information or leisure materials. In that regard, the library service is judged by results. How quickly and how well a user's needs are satisfied matter - and not how it was achieved.

Many submissions to the project team called for improvements in these areas, including a call for 'a truly national library service with its catalogue on-line and with all local branches able to process inter-library loans (while keeping all the branches that presently exist at local level). Let the National Library (or some other centre) keep an excellent general reference section, with open stacks and photocopy machines freely available for self-service copying. Those of us who live far from Dublin must be able to copy materials to take away with us!' [xliv]

As the scale of publishing expands and as its range diversifies, each library service in Ireland cannot now hope to stock everything that its users require. By applying market-research techniques, it should nevertheless be able to stock a substantial part of material that is most in demand and to give direct access to more material.

However, a large part of material that may be demanded and ought to be available will not be held on-site and needs to be brought in on request. This involves co-operation with other libraries and information services. The project team believes it is vital that co-operative arrangements with other libraries and other information-suppliers are as efficient as possible. Users, particularly of smaller libraries, understand the limitations of each library and can be reasonably expected to accept a lapse of time in providing certain materials. However, the project team believes that users can also reasonably expect that this period is as short as possible and is accurately estimated in advance.

The project team believes that public libraries should contribute to co-operative service provision in such a way as to provide the best service to the library user. Local delivery of the library service should continue to mask the processes behind it which embrace co-operation at national level and also with library services in Northern Ireland and in Britain. In order to enhance the level of co-operation, the following issues should be considered:

- networking strategies for public libraries overall
- the relationship of these to local authority networking strategies
- regional co-operation, local co-operation, cross-sector co-operation and co-operation in subject or special interest groupings
- the position of public libraries in relation to other parts of the library and information sector and also in relation to the Information Society Commission initiatives and policies.

The function of the library co-operation strategy should be to analyse and research the wealth of library and information resources available through all outlets funded publicly, privately and through the voluntary and community sector. These outlets should include academic and specialised libraries, the resources of the public library services and all other information services. In order to minimise the unnecessary duplication of effort required in the provision of these library and information services, agreement should be reached at county and city level on how this information can be stored and accessed and where the primary responsibilities for certain resources will lie. A designated officer at county or city level should be required to co-ordinate this approach and to meet with the appropriate agencies with a view to reaching a consensus on how this optimisation of resources will be achieved.

Negotiating change in how the obstacles to access are removed requires a sensitivity and generosity to all partners in this exercise. Areas of information where particular growth is foreseen include:

- health,
- business,
- law,
- entitlements,
- agriculture,
- EU and
- education.

Within the emerging information society in Ireland, growing quantities of information are stored in networks or in other digital forms and access must be guaranteed. The project team believes that public libraries must play their part by acting as a bridge between both the traditional information media and the new media, thereby enabling them to complement rather than exclude each other. The libraries can meet the disparate needs for knowledge through their large network of service points in association with all the information providers. In this way, the library is a central social forum for the community where information and activities can be combined in a spirit of community development.

The opening up of electronic networks between public and other library services and between public libraries and other agencies will be supported through ensuring compatibility of standards and eliminating other barriers to access. An Chomhairle Leabharlanna, as the advisory body to local authorities should assist in this approach and liaise with all authorities, as appropriate.

Information available on relevant electronic databases held in these networks includes information on stock, on the contents of the stock and electronic information services. The opportunities exist for affording equal access to this information through both subsidy by the library authority for costed services and through the provision for more direct links within the appropriate agencies for both costed and non-costed services

.

Recommendations:

The project team recommends that library authorities move rapidly towards implementing a network for resource-sharing. As a first step, a nation-wide sharing of catalogue data, using the measures recommended for ICT development, should be put in place.

The project team is not in a position to recommend on a particular technical approach to how catalogue data can be shared but it is strongly of the view that it must take place urgently and that every library user should have access to every catalogue.

The world of information is now too large for library authorities to exist on their own. They must engage in shared resources with all other library and information services. In this regard, the project team endorses the recommendations of the Committee on Library Co-operation (COLICO) report on Resource Sharing in Irish Libraries, published in September 1996.[xlv]

The COLICO report goes beyond the issue of sharing library materials and inter-library loans. It also addresses the sharing of resources such as staff, training and conservation measures. The following table sets out the opinions of 31 public librarians, on an all-Ireland basis, on a range of such issues:

Resource Sharing Activity	Participate Now (April 1996)	Would be Useful
Co-operative access to catalogues	9	17
Co-operative access to stock	7	14
Co-operative training	6	19
Exchange of staff	3	11
Co-operative acquisition	3	6
Co-operative conservation measures	1	12

The project team believes that the gap between actuality and aspiration must be bridged. It also believes that the impetus for co-operation must also come from library authorities. It cannot be imposed from the centre.

7.7.3 Co-operation with other local services

Co-operation for libraries does not stop with their relationship with other libraries or information services. The project team believes that if libraries wish to be part of the community, they must actively participate in, and offer support to, initiatives designed for the common good. The project team believes it is a matter for each library authority to devise how best it can make a contribution to the local community and at what level. The library input may range from making space available for a once-off exhibition to a structured involvement with major enterprise development projects.

The project team has identified two major channels through which this co-operation should flow. The first is co-operation with information suppliers and other relevant organisations who will help the library deliver a better information service to the public. The second channel comprises the library bringing its information base and information skills to the assistance of organisations or projects that are of benefit to the community. These may be volunteer, state or commercially-based organisations or projects. The level of involvement by the library with each may also vary.

With initiatives surrounding the first channel, it is more likely that the library will be a leading player in the co-operation. With those surrounding the second channel, the library is more likely to be in a support role.

In determining the exact range and depth of co-operation, the library should at all times seek out possible synergy between its resources and objectives and those of the co-operating partners. Each co-operative venture should respect issues of complementarity and subsidiarity. The COLICO report on Resource Sharing in Irish Libraries sets out a useful structure for assessing co-operative activities. In Section 5.9, it suggests four types of network and mutual support groups as follows:

Sectoral networks and groups.
Area-based networks and groups.
Subject-based networks and groups.
Technology-based networks and groups.

While the COLICO report uses these headings to assess co-operation between libraries and between libraries and information services, it also provides a useful matrix for library authorities to assess the full extent of its co-operative arrangements. Non-library partners might include:

Sectoral: Local\Regional Authority, Arts Council, Heritage Council

Area-Based: FAS, LEADER, ADM\Enterprise Board, Local Voluntary Organisations

Subject-Based: Local History Group, Local Environmental Organisations\ENFO\EPA, Writers Groups

Technology-Based: Internet User-Groups, Remote subject-based organisations.

Many of these co-operative arrangements are already set out in library authority development programmes. However, the project team believes that the arrangements in place for libraries to co-operate with organisations other than libraries would benefit from a critical examination by each library authority.

Recommendation:

The project team recommends that each library authority should determine for itself the range, nature, objectives and level of co-operation it proposes to have with other organisations in the locality, whether at branch or library authority level. A framework of co-operation should then be compiled in respect of each library authority which documents the nature of co-operation. It should be included in the co-operation strategy for the library authority.

The areas of education and of arts and culture are traditionally ones where the public library has traditionally been seen to have a strong role. In order to build a strong matrix of co-operative arrangements, the project team believes that these areas merit special attention.

• **Education**

The educational role of public libraries has been growing rapidly in the last decade. Areas of growth include new ways of service delivery and new thinking in promoting concepts of learning as opposed to formal education. Growing demands on library services are foreseen in the following areas:

Lifelong Learning Concepts.
Adult Literacy and Basic Skills.
ICT and Information-handling Skills
Further Education.
Open and Distance Learning and other appropriate initiatives of training and education.

In order to deliver the libraries' part in this process, strategic alliances and partnerships are required in a similar way to those in the information field. These would be with bodies such as the VEC's, National Adult Literacy Agency, FAS, local educational institutions and national support agencies.

Recommendation:

The project team recommends that a local strategy for developing co-operation with other educational services should be incorporated into the library co-operation strategy. An Chomhairle Leabharlanna, in association with the Department of Education and Science should support and assist this process.

• **Arts and culture**

The public library service is one of the primary cultural networks in Ireland. Relationships for programmes and strategies already exist between library authorities, local authority arts services and a wide range of art activists flourishing at local level, and also with the Arts Council, Creative Arts For

Everyone (CAFE) and other national institutions such as the Irish Museum of Modern Art (IMMA), National Gallery and the National Library. An Chomhairle Leabharlanna has also been involved through the Public Libraries and the Arts project. The role of the public library in developing arts and culture is discussed in more detail in section 7.9.3, below.

Recommendation:

With the expansion and diversification of arts provision, both locally and nationally, the project team recommends that a national strategy on delivering the arts in a way that is accessible to the wider community than has been available heretofore, should be established. Such a strategy should take as its starting point the report of the Public Libraries and the Arts project.

7.7.4 Co-operation at EU and international level

Each member state of the EU and most other countries operate a system of public libraries. Many are run in a manner similar to Ireland. They are all grappling with the same issues as we move further into the information age.

"Irish public libraries have much to learn from best practice in other countries and also have much to show in return"

It is clear to the project team that Irish public libraries have much to learn from best practice in other countries and also have much to show in return.

This is recognised at EU level as the European Commission promotes a programme of co-operation and exchange between libraries in areas such as ICT applications in public libraries, promotion of reading and writing through public libraries, promotion of arts and culture and integration of library services with distance learning programmes.

Many Irish public libraries have participated in one or more international projects under EU programmes and these have, in the main, been rewarding. There are costs associated with such participation, particularly in relation to staff time and it is not always clear if the identifiable benefits justify the cost. An Chomhairle Leabharlanna through its work as a focal point for the EU Framework Research Programmes, known as EuroFocus for Libraries, does important work in raising awareness and providing information on EU co-operative opportunities.

However, the international dimension to library co-operation is not confined to EU programmes. Many library authorities have engaged in co-operative ventures with other public library services on a bi-lateral or multi-lateral basis. Many of these occur as part of a more general co-operation between local authorities as part of a town-twinning process; others are as a result of formal or informal initiatives with library services in Northern Ireland. One example of international co-operation is the Annual International Poetry Festival organised by Dun Laoghaire-Rathdown Public Libraries. Another is the Annual International IMPAC Dublin Literary Award, now in its fourth year, which attracts entries from libraries all around the world.

Snap Shot: *Dun Laoghaire International Poetry Competition and Festival*

The Comórtas Filíochta/International Poetry Competition and Féile Filíochta are organised and operated by the Dun Laoghaire-Rathdown County Council Public Library Service, and are held annually.

They contribute to and take advantage of the multilingual and multicultural setting of the new emerging Europe. The events are local, national and European and promote the poetry and music of Europe in the form of open competition and performance.

Events are held strictly in accordance with the philosophy of the public library service which is to promote and facilitate the intellectual, recreational, and literary and cultural development of the individual and society. In harmony with this spirit there are no charges, as few rules and regulations as possible, events are open to adults and young people and they are organised and presented by the library staff with extensive outside co-operation.

The Comórtas Filíochta/International Poetry Competition is in eight languages English, Irish, German, French, Italian, Welsh, Spanish and Scottish Gaelic and has the support of a very wide number of bodies in Ireland and outside it, who present trophies and give other types of assistance.

The library prize-money this year will be £7,000. The Comórtas Filíochta/ International Poetry Competition has attracted entrants from throughout the whole of Ireland, Britain, the rest of Europe and beyond over the years.

The Comórtas Filíochta is followed by the Féile Filíochta which is a festival of poetry, music and dance. The main event of the Féile Filíochta is "Fionna Féile" which is the presentation of prizes evening at which the prize-winners are presented with their prizes and trophies by An Chathaoirleach, Dun Laoghaire- Rathdown County Council and by the representatives of supporting bodies.

The prize-winners in each section read their poems in the different languages and there is also a musical dimension to the evening. Throughout the week different events are held and over the years well known poets have taken part e.g. John F. Deane, Eavan Boland, Nuala Ní Dhomhnaill, Marie Mhac an tSaoi, Brian Lynch, Ted McNulty and others.

The week is rounded off by the "Read Your Own Poems in Public" evening at which the public are invited to read their own poems in the presence of an established poet who also gives a reading. The event is also interspersed with music.

What began as a small and very local poetry event ten years ago has now become international. It has been very successful and has massive potential - indeed its problems are related to its success.

Snap Shot: *International IMPAC Dublin Literary Award*

The International IMPAC Dublin Literary Award was founded in 1995 as an initiative of Dublin City Council in partnership with IMPAC, the international productivity improvement company whose European headquarters is based in Dublin. The aims of the Award are to promote Dublin internationally as a literary city; to promote library co-operation on an international scale; to bring excellent literature, including literature in translation, to the attention of library users in Dublin and abroad; and to give recognition to excellence in creative writing, translating, and publishing.

The Award is administered by Dublin City Public Library Service and the process is as follows:

public library services in selected cities around the world make nominations of novels for the award;

the nominated books are considered by an international panel of judges;

a short list of contenders for the award is announced in March each year;

the winner is announced in May each year;

the prize is presented to the winner in June each year, during Bloomstime.

The success of the Award depends on the co-operation of participating libraries which has, to date, been excellent. In the first year nominations were received from over 100 libraries and this level of participation has been maintained in the two succeeding years.

Each library included on the "active" database (197 in total) receives information on the short-list and winner on the afternoon of each announcement. The increasing use of E-mail means that, beginning this year, information will be sent out electronically (where possible). It has been found that the listing of nominated titles is very popular among libraries as it provides a unique list of recommended fiction, including books in English translation which might not otherwise come to the attention of acquisitions staff. Libraries also use the posters, which are designed and printed to a high standard, in literature promotions and exhibitions.

Some of Dublin Corporation Public Libraries' Internet home pages are devoted to the award, and these pages are used to provide updated information on a regular basis. Since 1997 a list of participating libraries with links to their web sites has been included on the pages. This listing provides an excellent resource for browsers seeking library contacts in over 50 countries world-wide.

Dublin Corporation Public Libraries is developing an Award collection, consisting of copies of every nominated title. This collection is set to become one of the finest collections of international fiction available and will be a great asset to the library service and its users.

The Award nominating process has led to inter-library co-operation on a huge scale and this co-operation has and will provide opportunities for Dublin Corporation and its staff to engage in further inter-library projects with colleagues around the world.

The international dimension of public libraries does not always involve co-operation with other library services. A number of Irish libraries have benefited from funding from UNESCO, which has enabled them to carry out work on their collections that would not have been otherwise possible.

While the project team acknowledges the efforts made by library authorities to include an international dimension in their programmes, it also notes the constraints that there are in this area.

Apart from not being able to devote resources to this area, the project team believes that the missing ingredient in many cases is information. Many library authorities do not have the information or awareness of the international opportunities that are available or do not have an international network of contacts to access. In particular, where Irish libraries have a problem to solve or indeed an innovative solution to offer, it is often not possible to look to the international arena to receive or offer assistance.

Accordingly, the project team believes that a clearing-house for international opportunities and international contacts should be developed by An Chomhairle Leabharlanna, which would go beyond the remit of the current EuroFocus focal point. The project team believes that there is an important role for an advisory service to library authorities that can provide guidance on the international dimension of public libraries. This would not just be confined to one aspect of public libraries or to one geographical area but would generate a knowledge base on international library developments that can be applied in Ireland.

It should also become a focal point for public libraries or other bodies at international level wishing to make contact with Irish public libraries. A related aspect to library development is the contribution that Irish public libraries can make to the development of public libraries in an international, particularly EU, context. In that regard, the project team acknowledges the work of PubliCA, EBLIDA and other international organisations working to promote and develop public libraries.

In particular, the project team endorses the communiqué issued in August this year by senior public library managers from 23 European countries, gathered in Leuven, Belgium, at a workshop organised by

PubliCA. The project team believes that the findings and recommendations in this report concord with the contents of the Leuven communiqué in terms of supporting democracy and citizenship; economic and social development; lifelong learning and cultural and linguistic diversity. The project team recognises that Irish public libraries have a role to play in shaping the future of public libraries at EU level and encourages the greatest degree of participation in appropriate fora.

Recommendation

The project team recommends that the remit, composition and services of EuroFocus on Libraries be expanded to embrace all levels and sectors of international library co-operation. EuroFocus should be seen as a pro-active element in an overall advisory service provided to library authorities.

Notes

xliv   Submission from Ms. Sharon Corcoran, Carlow.

xlv   White B. Resource Sharing in Irish Libraries: Report to An Chomhairle Leabharlanna (COLICO), 1996

7.8.1 General

The project team believes that the public library has a positive contribution to make to the formal education system in Ireland. In particular, the team believes that the library can assist in the development of literacy and reading and in the development of information skills amongst schoolgoers.

The project team strongly believes that this contribution is best made by well-resourced school libraries at both primary and post-primary levels.

7.8.2 Literacy and reading

Recent international studies[xlvi] have detected two main findings in relation to literacy and reading in Ireland:

- Irish children are above the OECD average for reading skills at age 9, but below average at age 14.

- 25% of Irish people have literacy problems.

The problems, which these disturbing findings illustrate, have more than one cause, which go beyond the effectiveness of schools in teaching basic skills and embrace a wide range of social, economic and cultural issues. The project team believes, however, that school libraries can help tackle the problem. At primary level, the library service is already involved, as an agent for the Department of Education and Science, in supplying library materials to schools. This service is quite successful and has benefited from increased funding in recent years. However, the current rate of support of approximately £2.12 per pupil is still inadequate to meet the need for high-quality materials.

The relationship at local level between librarians and school managers varies throughout the country. In some places there is a high level of co-operation and synergy between the schools and the library. In others, the enthusiasm for co-operation is less.

In order to overcome the difficulties with this haphazard approach, the project team believes that a national approach to developing schools libraries at primary level needs to be taken. As one submission to the project stated: "having a library in a school should be like having glasses of water in a restaurant".[xlvii] Other submissions on this topic called for a specially-trained liaison librarian for schools.

In that regard, the project team welcomes the establishment of the Primary School Library Research Project by the Library Association of Ireland (LAI) with funding from the Department of Education and Science. The project will:

- identify the current level of information resource provision within primary schools nation-wide;
- identify future requirements for resource provision and management within primary schools;
- ascertain the ability to source and manage information on the part of pupils and teachers;
- make recommendations for future access to information and its utilisation in primary schools.

The project team believes the outcome of this project will be important in shaping future schools library services.

Recommendation:

In order to accelerate the development of schools libraries, the project team recommends to the Minister that he facilitate a dialogue between library authorities, An Chomhairle Leabharlanna, the Department of the Environment and Local Government and the Department of Education and Science. This dialogue would consider how best schools libraries might develop and would take account of the issues arising for all parties.

In addition to issues raised by the LAI project, the parties might consider the proposal for a Schools Library Information File, already put forward by the Library Association of Ireland. This file would assist schools in setting up libraries and in running them effectively. The file would contain an easy-to-use guide to the technical and policy issues surrounding the development of school libraries.

The project team believes that schools libraries at post-primary level are less well-developed than at primary level. The team believes that a re-evaluation of how these services are delivered and financed needs to take place. The team believes that the public library service can contribute to post-primary schools library development by making qualified and experienced librarians available to advise schools managers on library development and best practise. Likewise, the team believes that there are major benefits to be obtained for pupils from a structured approach to co-operation that results in better library services being made available to them.

Recommendation:

The project team recommends to the Minister that he facilitate a dialogue between library authorities, An Chomhairle Leabharlanna, the Department of Environment and Local Government and the Department of Education and Science on the development of post-primary schools library services.

7.8.3 Information skills

The project team believes that the resources of the library service can help make the study and acquisition of information skills a success in Irish schools. In that regard, the project team notes the work carried out by Transition Year Support Team and Dun Laoghaire Youth Information Centre, funded by the Department of Education and Science, in developing a module on Information Studies for Transition Year Studies.

The project team agrees with the authors' conclusions that information skills "are important basic skills which will act as foundations on which problem solving behaviour may develop and grow to meet future life challenges, whether in the student's education, career or personal life. They are survival skills for the information age...[and]... may make all the difference between a fulfilled, productive life and mere existence."[xlviii]

By co-operating with schools and Youth Information Centres, the library can provide the practical hands-on approach to information handling that students need.

Recommendation:

The project team recommends that librarians should familiarise themselves with the contents of the module on Information Studies for Transition Year Studies, work actively with teachers implementing the module and also promote the concept of information studies in their other contacts with schools.

Notes

vi   Enter details of UNESCO study etc.

xlvii   Submission from Mr. D. McGinley, Letterkenny, Donegal

xlviii Information Studies, Transition Year Support Team, Blackrock Education Centre, 1998, p10

7.9.1 General

There is an ambiguity about culture which suggests that a thesaurus might be better used in its definition than a dictionary. A selection of synonyms for culture includes: enlightenment, enrichment, erudition, learning and civilisation. In the context of this report, however, culture may be defined as the process by which society's intellectual endeavours are recorded, preserved and promoted.

This process becomes a knowledge base and a record of cultural experience which links the past with present and future initiative and helps provide a community with a sense of its cultural identity. This knowledge base is comprised not only of the collections in a library, which are available for loan but also includes:

- Genealogical records
- Local studies and administrative archival collections
- Community information
- Art objects
- Music
- Foreign literature and language collections
- Map collections
- Photographic material
- Political literature
- Ephemeral collections of posters, postcards and playbills
- Business records

As a custodian of these records of cultural identity at both local and national levels, the public library plays a significant role in developing Irish culture. The public library also plays a significant and unique role in facilitating public access to the diversity of cultural experience which exists outside of Ireland.

"Regardless of developments in relation to information and communication technology, the cultural roles and cultural resources of the library are of paramount importance"

The project team underlines the importance of the cultural role of the public library for the people of Ireland. Regardless of developments in relation to information and communication technology, the cultural roles and cultural resources of the library are of paramount importance. The project team believes strongly that access to cultural resources is consistent with the needs of life-long-learning and democratisation within the context of an inclusive society.

To a large extent the library can meet the need simply by being there, being open, facilitating access and investing in library materials. In this way, the contents of each library can be a treasure-house for the library-user.

One submission to the project team elaborated on the role that the library had played in her cultural development. She wrote: "My most depressing memory of growing up in the country in Co. Leitrim and listening to Michael O'Hehir's voice on Sunday afternoons and me bored with very little to read, apart from the Sunday Press and the Leitrim Observer. Living on a farm, it was unheard of to waste time reading books....When I moved to Sligo, I joined the library and from that time onwards my life changed...I got buried in Mary Lavin's short stories, Somerville and Ross and Annie M.P. Smithson along with Canon Sheehan and Frank O'Connor's books.....

I had a holiday in Dusseldorf last year and I came on the work of the poet Heinrich Heine... I came upon a wonderful exhibition of his work through paintings made up by several schools in France and Germany. I knew no German but I could follow much of the stories through the paintings....

I have been writing poetry since the late 1970's and have had poems included in several anthologies. My latest poem published happens to have the title 'In the Library'..."[xlix]

This experience is not unusual, yet far more frequent is the contribution that public libraries make to an individual's appreciation and understanding of cultural matters. This may not be reflected in their lives as directly as in the submission above, but will certainly make a difference to their quality of life.

The importance of the library to cultural development is recognised by others, including the Arts Council, who state in the Arts Plan that " The extensive public library system constitutes (with RTE) the most important cultural network in the country, being also the single greatest purchaser of books."[1]

At the same time, the project team believes that the cultural network of libraries is unevenly developed. Most library authorities take a very positive and proactive approach to cultural development and are coming from a background in which cultural collections were the bedrock of the library. They operate in different ways however, with some focusing on developing high-quality collections and others emphasising an activity-based approach. A library authority's approach to cultural development is generally in line with its overall approach to the library service. It is also influenced by the level and nature of support available for cultural development at both national and local levels and also reflects the level and nature of public demand.

7.9.2 Accessing cultural resources

The project team believes that there are serious issues to be addressed in releasing the cultural value in each library to the greatest number of people. Many of those are related to the general issues of availability, accessibility and quality of library services outlined earlier in this chapter. Others are more specialist and relate to mechanisms to allow greater use to be made of collections that are necessarily confined to one physical location.

As with other areas of library service, the quality of staff available in libraries is of vital importance. Staff members who know and understand the cultural value of the material in their care will be better able to guide and advise library users. library authorities traditionally have in their number, staff members who have an authoritative knowledge and a deep understanding and appreciation of what the library holds and are dedicated to its conservation, dissemination and promotion. However, this has mainly occurred as a result of personal interest and

research. The project team believes that the training of library staff should include elements that relate to developing specialist knowledge about collections of high value and how the collections can be optimised for public access.

Recommendation:

The project team recommends that all library staff should have a detailed knowledge of cultural resources available. This should be developed as an integrated part of the Library Staff Development Plan outlined earlier in this report.

Training measures in this area should be accompanied by a staff mobility policy aimed at extending public access to specialist knowledge throughout the library area of responsibility. This policy may include placements or staff-exchanges with other cultural institutions such as museums or archives.

"New technology also offers the library new opportunities to make greater use of its collections"

New technology also offers the library new opportunities to make greater use of its collections. Some of these are discussed in relation to the general development of ICT infrastructure in libraries. However some other applications are of particular relevance in relation to delivering access to the cultural assets of libraries. The project team believes that significant efforts should be made to extend the reach of the libraries collections by digitising items of particular value and by using ICT to promote awareness of the valuable items held in public libraries. In particular, the following measures should be considered:

- creation of a national on-line network for local studies which takes advantage of the increased use of ICT in Irish libraries, and would lead to the provision of full networked bibliographic information on local studies materials in all formats, accessible in all libraries and via the Internet.

- a programme of digitisation of local studies materials, beginning with unique / rare resources, but with the long term aim of making the holdings of all local studies sections available in digitised form. Local studies material which might be reproduced in digital form would include photographs and prints, historic maps, local newspapers, community information, leaflets, rare printed material, archival and genealogical resources.

- a programme of conservation and preservation. The combined local studies collections of Irish public libraries are an irreplaceable national resource, and there is a need for greater concentration on the conservation of original materials, given the increasing pressure on such unique resources held in local studies collections. Investment in conservation and in digitisation together would mean that unique and at risk items would rarely if ever need to be made available for consultation.

- a series of publications by local authorities aimed at promoting local studies, initially targeted at innovative projects. This would include the publication, in print or electronic form, of bibliographies and finding aids, as well as reproductions of rare works and the results of new research. Investment would also support the production and publication of interactive local studies products, such as CD-ROM's, local studies learning packages related to family history and specific towns/parishes.

The project team recognises that the suggested measures are commonly faced by other cultural institutions such as the National Archives, National Library, Royal Irish Academy and many more at national and local level. Accordingly, the project team believes a national programme that would be open to all institutions is perhaps the most cost-effective way forward.

Such a programme should come under the aegis of the Department of Arts, Heritage, Gaeltacht and the Islands and might form part of an international approach to cultural development which might seek support through the EU and/or UNESCO

Recommendations:
The project team recommends to the Minister that he request the Minister for Arts, Heritage, Gaeltacht and the Islands to initiate a national programme to apply the benefits of ICT to library collections of high cultural value.

This initiative should also involve other bodies with a role to play, such as the National Library, National Archives, Arts Council and the Heritage Council.

The programme should address issues of:

- conservation;
- security;
- promotion of access;
- creation of cultural content;
- publication of material in electronic formats locally, nationally and via the world-wide web;
- research on innovative content-based service initiatives utilising web-based information technologies.

7.9.3 Using library resources to promote culture

The project team also believes that existing avenues for the promotion of culture should make greater use of material held in public libraries and services offered by public libraries. In particular, the project team is concerned by the "dumbing-down" of the mass media, with items of cultural value being diluted and repackaged as entertainment. The project team believes that material available through the library service can be a useful antidote to this trend. However, in order to promote awareness of what the library service offers, it is necessary to have a presence with broadcasters and publishers.

Given the exponential growth in broadcasting capacity offered by digital technology, and the development of local radio, the project team believes that consideration be given to the contribution that the library can make to the promotion of access to cultural material through the mass media. This may take the format of producing packages of content for use in television and radio programmes or even the production of specific Library Television programmes.

The content of such packages and programmes would be based on library collections and activities such as exhibition, lectures, demonstrations, recitals, readings, book discussions and storytelling.

Recommendation:

The project team recommends that An Chomhairle Leabharlanna, in association with a selection of library authorities and broadcasters should research the costs and benefits of generating a greater public library presence in the mass media, focused on providing greater access to cultural resources held in the public library.

7.9.4 The public library service as an agent for arts and heritage development.

Two other issues of particular relevance to the development of libraries' cultural role are:

- defining the role of public libraries in the arts
- defining the role of public libraries in relation to local and national heritage.

"local authorities are important players in the field of arts development"

Public Libraries and the Arts

In addition to the services offered through public libraries, local authorities are important players in the field of arts development. In times past, this took a physical form such as municipal galleries or local authority art collections. In recent years, local authority intervention in the arts has been augmented by the engagement of Arts Officers to deliver a programme of arts activities and events. These posts and some of the programmes are jointly funded by the Arts Council. Arts Officers are now widely established in local authorities and a style of arts programme, which generally focuses on popular participation in the arts is becoming evident. Local authority management and local authority members are increasingly aware of the benefit of arts programmes, particularly as an aid to local development and community development.

At the same time, the project team recognises that the position and structure of the arts programme in local authorities should be examined. This particularly includes the relationship that should exist between the arts and the library services.

In that regard, the Arts Plan recommended co-operation between the Arts Council and An Chomhairle Leabharlanna to expand co-operation in the field of arts and libraries. In order to develop the best strategy for co-operation between libraries and the arts, a major study was undertaken by a committee drawn from all relevant sectors.

The study found that:

- The public library service is seen as an exceptionally appropriate host for community arts activities.

- The success of libraries and of local authority arts activities have had in providing positive and life-enhancing experiences for the community suggests that there is a very strong foundation for co-operation between the two services.

- Any co-operative arrangements must also recognise the differences which exist between the two services in relation to culture, training, strategic objectives and day-to-day focus.

- Library infrastructure is not generally suitable for arts activities without adjustments. Restricted availability is also a hindrance to co-operation.

- There are deficiencies in library collections, particularly in relation to literature for young adults, Irish language literature and specialist arts materials.

- There are opportunities for co-operation between arts and libraries and more importantly for joint co-operation with a wide range of other agencies and groups.

- Participation by libraries in arts activities will raise the profile of libraries and will enhance the position of the arts in the community.

The project team endorses these findings and supports measures that will lead to greater co-operation between both library and arts services.

The project team believes that the next Arts Plan offers an opportunity for the Arts Council to propose new approaches in which the library service can help develop the arts in Ireland in a way that embraces all art-forms and looks beyond the obvious art-form of literature.

Recommendation:

The project team recommends that the Arts Council, in formulating and in implementing the next Arts Plan, should take account of the positive role that libraries can play in developing the full spectrum of the arts in Ireland. This is particularly important for communities that do not have access to any other arts infrastructure.

Snap Shot: *Libraries and Arts in Donegal*

The Central Library & Arts Centre in Letterkenny, Co. Donegal is now into its fourth year of operation.

The construction and fitting-out was jointly funded by the Department of the Environment, the Department of Arts, Culture and the Gaeltacht (as it was then called), and Donegal County Council. In keeping with its vision for the centre, the Council made generous provision for public art, commissioning a wall hanging by Rosemary McCarron and poems by internationally known Gaelic language poet Cathal Ó Searcaigh and local English language poet Frank Galligan. In 1997, to mark the 75th anniversary of the establishment of the library service in Donegal, the Council commissioned Aileen Barr to make and install a series of ceramic works placed in the pavement around the building.

The Central Library is the flagship of the library service, and houses the Donegal Local Studies collection, and the main Reference and Business Information points in the county. It also serves the largest population centre in Donegal; more than 10,000 children and adults have joined the library and regularly borrow books, CDs, videos and other media.

The Arts Centre hosts a varied programme of exhibitions and concerts, by touring artists (from as far away as the Cape Verde Islands) and people from the area, as well as being used, for an average of 60 hours each week, by community arts groups - workshops, meetings and classes in every artform from painting, modern dance, and rock music to set-dancing. It was the venue used by the Arts Council in September 1998 for their public consultation process in the North-West.

It is in the cross-fertilisation between the library and the arts, however, that the centre has really come into its own; strengthening the library's role as the key agency in fostering local cultural expression, and encouraging a whole new audience - the library's users - to participate in the arts. The library staff actively encourage people to visit exhibitions and attend gigs/performances, and the feeling that 'the arts are not for me', which is often a major obstacle to participation, is gradually being broken down.

Public libraries and local and national heritage.

Public libraries have, since their establishment, been to the fore in promoting interest, education, knowledge and pride in our heritage. They also have facilitated the appreciation and enjoyment of heritage by the public and have co-operated with other organisations with similar objectives.

In practical terms, this has meant that libraries, particularly in their local studies collections have developed significant holdings of important heritage value. These holdings go beyond books or manuscripts and in many locations include collections that could equally be held in museums.

In more recent years, there have been developments in relation to local authority archives and museums as well as local genealogy projects. The development of these specialised services, mandatory in the case of local authority archives, poses new challenges to the library service. In addition, libraries are also designated as venues for reference to local sites and monuments records and for exhibiting details of Special Areas of Conservation.

Snap Shot: *Family History in Leitrim County Library*

Over the past fifteen years the local studies section at the County Library in Ballinamore, has expanded and developed its family history/genealogy services through the use of FAS schemes.

Work on indexing genealogy record started in 1983. The variety of sources which have been indexed and computerised include:

- Church Records
  All registers of baptism, marriage and death, for all parishes in Co. Leitrim, for all religions have been indexed and computerised up to 1900.

- Graveyard Inscriptions
  A project providing unique information was a survey of all graveyards in Leitrim, producing maps showing headstones and tomb stones. Inscriptions were transcribed and indexes to names were also produced.

- Genealogy Service
  Since 1986 a full-time genealogy service has been provided. A new building was opened in 1994 for the service.

- Other Sources
  Additional information is provided through computerisation of Griffith's Valuation, 1901 Census and civil records of marriages and births.

- Newspaper Indexing
  Most of the Leitrim papers up to 1905 have now been indexed. Indexing is very detailed. Up to eight people have been engaged in this project since it started about ten years ago.

- Interviewing Old People
  Over two hundred people have been interviewed over the past 7-8 years. These interviews are now being transcribed and typed up. They are a very valuable source for family, local and national history.

Family history reports are researched and produced and fees are charged in line with Irish Family History Foundation policy. The service is run by a limited company but is supervised by the Co. Librarian. Apart from FAS, funding has been received from Ireland Funds, International Fund for Ireland, Programme for Peace and Reconciliation.

These developments can however lead to difficulties and a confusion of roles. The library service is seen by many local authorities as an overall management structure for heritage services. For example, the report of the Steering Group on Local Authority Records and Archives[li] saw the need for continuing involvement of the library service in relation to archives. It recommended that the local archives service should operate within the library service. In addition, it recommended that libraries and archives should share accommodation where appropriate.

"the library service should develop a strong co-operation with local archives, museum and genealogy services - whether within or outside the local authority"

This view of the library service is not always shared by others. However, it is not an issue upon which the project team feels it appropriate to make specific recommendations. In general terms, the project team believes that the library service should develop a strong co-operation with local archives, museum and genealogy services - whether within or outside the local authority. The precise nature and structure of the co-operation is something to be developed locally and should respect fully the separate specialisms of cognate professionals.

The advantage for the library of a close relationship with other heritage services will be in delivering a better service to the public by being able to deal with general queries directly and by referring library-users to a specialist service when appropriate. The advantage to archives, museums and genealogy services will be in increasing the number of customers using their service and also in having the library deal directly with more straightforward queries etc. The scope of the co-operation can also extend to areas such as hosting exhibitions, jointly organising public courses, staff training, sharing of non-specialist staff, joint marketing initiatives and sharing databases and catalogues.

The project team recognises that the development of Ireland's heritage goes well beyond the public library service and embraces a wide range of organisations. The project team welcomes the initiative of the Minister for Arts, Culture, Gaeltacht and the Islands in commissioning a National Heritage Plan. As a nation-wide, democratically-accountable, locally-based cultural service, the public library has a lot to contribute to the formulation and subsequent implementation of the National Heritage Plan. The project team believes that each library authority should contribute to the plan in whatever way it deems appropriate. The project team also feels that a single submission from the public library service would be useful in order to deal with issues of common concern.

Recommendations:

The project team recommends that library authorities participate fully in the preparation of the National Heritage Plan.

The project team also recommends that An Chomhairle Leabharlanna should co-ordinate a submission to the Department of Arts, Heritage, Gaeltacht and the Islands concerning the plan. The submission should be prepared in consultation with a representative group of librarians. An Chomhairle Leabharlanna should also act as an on-going point of contact for the Department of Arts, Heritage, Gaeltacht and the Islands during the preparation of the Plan.

Notes

xlix   *Submission from Ms. Mary Guckian, Dublin*

l   *The Arts Plan, 1995, p. 66*

li   *Report of Steering Group of Local Authority Records and Archives, Department of the Environment, April 1996, Chapters 6, 7*

ISSUE 9 Improving the service through library research

Earlier in this report, the issue of marketing public libraries is discussed and the need for research in order to market the service properly is stressed. However, the project team believes that the need for research extends well beyond the area of marketing and that it should underpin all aspects of the public library service.

The project team believes that research into issues of relevance to public libraries in Ireland is inadequate and needs to be improved. Likewise, the project team believes that best use is not being made of the research that is available.

There have been some noteworthy research projects carried out at local and national level which looked at issues such health information, literacy and reading and the role of public libraries and the arts. However, most of the research projects carried out by library authorities have tended to be applied research and have looked at areas such as the integration of library services with distance learning (LISTED) or on providing telematics-based library services for blind and visually-impaired readers (TESTLAB).

Projects such as these generally involve international partners and are part-funded by the EU. While the quality of the research is generally satisfactory, there are special difficulties generated in working with international partners. The experience has also been that the research has been made possible as a result of the existence of a wide-ranging EU programme of funding rather than as a result of a programme focused on libraries. This has resulted in an approach to topic selection which is orientated to match the objectives of the EU programme, rather than an approach designed to meet local priorities.

Snap Shot: LISTED Project

In late 1997, Naas Library was chosen as a test site for a EU funded research project called LISTED. This project investigates the integration of library services with distance learning. The major goal of the project is to develop an extended catalogue of open and distance learning materials and to make this available on the Internet.

In practical terms the effect on Naas Library was the installation of two new PCs, a laser printer and two Internet connections. A collection of tutorial CD-ROM's were purchased in a variety of subjects and a grant from Action South Kildare made possible the installation of two wheelchair-friendly IT learning units.

The target groups for the initial stage of the project were the unemployed, wheelchair users and people on return to work courses. Implementation of the project involved co-operation with the Irish Wheelchair Association Training Centre in Clane, the Naas Resource Centre for the Unemployed and the John Sullivan Centre in Clane.

The participants ranged in age from 20 to 50, were male and female and had various disabilities ranging from MS and Spina Bifida to stroke and head injury.

Feedback from the IWA reports a high level of satisfaction with the project - particular mention being made of the Internet as information and communication tool. As a result they now have Internet access in their centre. All of the participants would like to continue the project.

The whole project has been of enormous benefit to Naas Library, as it has allowed staff to further extend its existing services to marginalised section of the community, and is able to offer a new range of telematic services to them and other users. It has also boosted the enthusiasm of staff for the whole concept of telematic learning and an eagerness to expand the present range of services.

In addition to research carried out by library authorities, An Chomhairle Leabharlanna has been to the fore in carrying out and commissioning research into issues of common interest to all library authorities. Examples include an assessment of the issues surrounding the provision of Internet facilities in libraries and the development of an overall policy for the library and information services sector in Ireland. The results of these projects should be of benefit in a general way to all library authorities. The Library Association of Ireland has also been engaged in research. In addition to the current project concerning primary schools, it has completed research in relation to consumer health information and information services for medical staff. These projects received funding from the Department of Health and Children.

The impression remains however that library authorities encounter difficulties in carrying out research that is of specific use to them in delivering their services. There are also difficulties in accessing relevant research carried out elsewhere and in disseminating research that may have been carried out or commissioned by them.

"While library authorities generally support the concept of research, there is little evidence of library services being developed on the basis of a sound research project"

The project team believes that a lack of resources is the primary reason for the paucity of research. In this regard, libraries are no different from many other sectors, both public and private. Coupled with the lack of resources is a lack of appreciation for the value of research. While library authorities generally support the concept of research, there is little evidence of library services being developed on the basis of a sound research project.

In this regard, the Library Development Programmes, required of all library authorities under the Local Government Act, demanded some research by library authorities in their compilation. The available plans show a diverse range and quality of research undertaken. More seriously, there is little evidence of significant changes being made to library authority activities or services consequent on research carried out for those programmes.

The project team believes that research into issues affecting public libraries in Ireland has a lot to offer to the development of the service. Throughout this chapter the team has flagged areas of activity that it feels would benefit from research. In order to ensure that this research is carried out in the most effective manner, the project team believes that An Chomhairle should play a role in co-ordinating the commissioning of a research programme and the dissemination of its findings. However, the topics for research should be decided by a representative group drawn from public libraries and should focus on improving the public library service.

The following topics have already been indicated in this report as being suitable for research:

- Assessment of Open Learning Tools for library staff (7.2.2)
- Improving delivery of specialised services (7.2.4)
- Marketing of public libraries (7.6)
- Provision of library-based content to the mass media (7.9)
- Innovative service-delivery methods for isolated communities (7.4)

While the responsibility for developing the service through research lies with library authorities, the project team believes that the Minister should make a financial contribution to a research programme in order to overcome the paucity of resources referred to earlier. This contribution, which should be at least matched by library authorities should be seen as a short-term measure and should not extend beyond three years.

Recommendations:

In order to improve the research climate and by implication to improve the quality of library

services, the project team recommends that a co-ordinated approach to Irish public library research should be undertaken. This should be formalised as a Public Libraries Research Programme, with specific terms of reference and an identifiable budget.

The project team recommends that the design of the programme should be carried out by a representative group of public librarians and that its implementation should be co-ordinated by An Chomhairle Leabharlanna,

The co-ordination would also include the dissemination of relevant research to library authorities as well as the exploitation of research carried out by them.

The project team also recommends that a public library research fund should be established. This would be used to assist library authorities in carrying out research locally and in the commissioning of research from third parties. The annual funding requirement should be included as part of the funding levy for An Chomhairle Leabharlanna. The contribution from library authorities should be matched by the Department of the Environment and Local Government, while third-party contributions should also be sought.

eight

Next Steps

8

8.1 Introduction

The project team considers that the recommendations outlined in the previous chapter constitute an ambitious agenda for library development for the next 8 years.

8.2 Suggested steps

Implementation of the recommendations will require a significantly greater input of resources by all parties. Apart from financial resources, it is clear that significant staff resources will be required. Input will also be required to plan how the recommendations will be implemented, to oversee their implementation and to monitor progress.

The project team considers that recommendations on implementation mechanisms to be outside its terms of reference. However, it sets out below some suggestions as to the next steps that might be taken.

These suggestions are made on the assumption that the Minister accepts, at least in the main, the findings and recommendations of the review.

"The project team believes that a commitment from the Minister that significant extra funding will be available on a multi-annual basis for the development of the library service is the most important step that can be taken at this point"

The project team believes that a commitment from the Minister that significant extra funding will be available on a multi-annual basis for the development of the library service is the most important step that can be taken at this point. Such a commitment would be an important and positive signal to other stakeholders in the library service. It would also help unlock the commitment, financial and otherwise from those stakeholders that will be necessary for the successful implementation of the recommendations in this review.

The project team would also suggest to the Minister that, in addition to a commitment on funding, he might indicate his reaction to the other recommendations addressed to him and a timetable for implementing those which he accepts. Likewise library authorities, An Chomhairle Leabharlanna and others should outline their reaction to the recommendations made by the project team and how they foresee them being implemented..

It is proposed that the Department, in consultation with the other stakeholders in the public library service would then put in place a framework to oversee the general implementation of all the recommendations in the review. To initiate this process, the implementation framework should be the subject of a conference for all parties interested in the development of the public library service.

In the meantime, it is proposed that the Minister should make arrangements for the review of the Department's library investment programme to commence as soon as possible. This review should involve consultation with library authorities and An Chomhairle Leabharlanna.

It is also proposed that the Minister should make arrangements for a national approach to ICT provision in libraries to be developed as soon as possible. This should be carried out by the Department in consultation with An Chomhairle Leabharlanna, library authorities, the Local Government Computer Services Board, the Information Society Commission and telecommunications suppliers.

It is also proposed that An Chomhairle Leabharlanna propose to the Department a formula for allocating funds that the Minister may make available for funding stock in libraries.

nine

Acknowledgements

9

Acknowledgements:

The project team thank sincerely everybody who helped in carrying out the review of public library policy and in producing this report.

In particular the project team thanks the members of the public who took the time and made the effort to express their opinions of the public library service. The high number of submissions reflects the high regard that the public hold for what is, in effect, their library service.

The project team also thank everybody within the public library service and around it who contributed freely of their advice and who responded enthusiastically to requests for information, advice or other material.

The project team wishes to record its special appreciation of the contribution made to its work by Tim Mawe, who combined a deep knowledge and understanding of the subject matter with an ability to deliver drafts of high quality, even under considerable time-pressure. He was ably supported in this by the Secretary to the project team, Veronica Healy, who also organised and minuted project team meetings with great efficiency, and Kevin McCormick. Their unfailing helpfulness and enthusiasm ensured that the project team's work was as enjoyable as it was productive and the project team is grateful to all three.

AN ROINN COMHSHAOIL AGUS RIALTAIS ÁITIÚIL

**DEPARTMENT OF THE ENVIRONMENT
AND LOCAL GOVERNMENT**

HELP BUILD A BETTER PUBLIC LIBRARY SERVICE.

What do you think of the service provided by the public libraries in Ireland?

What do you need from the public library service?

How can the service be improved to meet your needs and those of the community in which you live?

If you have something to say on these issues, we would like to hear it.

We are a Project Team which has been set up by the Minister for the Environment and Local Government to review his Department's policy on public libraries and we want to know what the public feel about the library service.

We are looking at all aspects of the existing library service and at future trends that affect it.

We will report to the Minister during 1998 and will make recommendations to him on the development of the public library service.

Everyone is welcome to make a submission - whether they are library users or not. Submissions are welcome from individuals and from groups.

If you wish to make a submission to our work, you should send it to the Secretary to the Team (see below). It should reach us by 13 February 1998.

If you want to know more about the review, please contact:

Veronica Healy,
Secretary, Public Library
Policy Review Project,
Room 51,
Custom House, Dublin 1.

Telephone: (01) 6793377, ext. 2370
Fax: (01) 8742710
e-mail: Libpol@environ.irlgov.ie

Individuals who made submissions

Kitty Murphy, Cork City.

Michael Grogan, Offaly.

Richard Collins, Cork.

Maeve Coyle, Donegal.

Margaret Crinnion, Kildare.

Helen McCrarren, Monaghan.

Mary Guckian, Dublin.

Jeremiah Kennedy, Kerry.

Ingrid Barry, Cork.

Vincent & Ruth Hunt, Dublin.

Martina Prout, Waterford.

Mary Robinson, Dublin.

Lorraine Marshall, Cork.

Patrick Waters, Donegal.

Liam Geary, Kerry.

Anne O'Leary, Dublin.

Catriona Reid, Dublin.

Jean Curtin, Dublin.

Mary McConnon, Dundalk.

Patrick V. Kelly, Cork.

Fiona White, Kildare.

Gloria Hamilton, Kildare.

Eithne Connolly, Kildare.

Sylvia Julian, Kildare.

Ann O'Neill-Brown, Kildare.

Joe Rafferty, Galway.

Barbara Whelan, Dublin.

Anne O'Neill, Kildare.

Robert Norton, Dublin

Marian Gunning, Kerry.

Mrs. O'Dwyer, Tipperary.

Una McGrealy, Dublin.

Elizabeth O'Sullivan, Limerick.

J. Duane, Galway.

Rena Harford, Dublin.

Rose Pearce, Galway.

Tom Finn, Co. Kerry.

Pat Finn, Tipperary

Antoin Kiely, Clare.

Stephanie Walsh, Tipperary

Hazel Thompson, Dublin.

Sunniva O'Brien, Waterford.

Mervyn Groves, Clare.

Vivienne Flanagan, Dublin.

Jim Cummins, Kilkenny.

Carol Geraghty, Galway.

Bernie Caffrey, Kildare.

J. Leonard, Cork.

Sharon Corcoran, Carlow.

Cornelius F. Smith, Dublin.

M.J. Belford, Clare.

Deirdre Ryan, Tipperary.

Dermot Roche, Wexford.

Fergus Etchingham, Wicklow.

Noreen McMahon, Limerick.

Jim O'Brien, Meath.

Eileen McCormack, Kildare.

Orlaith Mannion, Galway.

Anne Foley, Kildare

Theresa M. Lee, Kildare.

Paul Murray, Dublin.

Josephine Keane, Wexford.

Brian McCabe, Kildare.

Justine Finn, Cork.

Mary Keely, Wexford.

Kenneth O'Loughlin, Clare.

Padraig O'Concubhair, Kerry.

Angela King, Dublin.

Mary Lehane, Cork.

Michael & Jo Kavanagh, Dublin.

Tony Deeney, Cork.

Eileen O'Connor, Limerick.

Larry Phillips, Limerick.

Vera Maye, Kerry.

Sarah Greene, Donegal.

Adrian Gebruers, Cork.

Michael Falvey, Clare.

Kay Lonergan, Tipperary.

Alice McDermott, Roscommon.

Graham W. Pearson, Laois.

Margaret Newcombe, Cork.

Geraldine Gormley, Sligo.

Margaret Hayden, Carlow.

Deirdre Curtin, Kildare.

Martin O'Loughlin, Tipperary.

Helen Kiernan, Dublin.

P.J. Kennedy, Cavan.

Catriona Kinane, Tipperary.

Anne Leech, Meath.

Anne Kearns, Dublin.

Adrienne Sullivan, Dublin.

Delia Butler-Toomey, Limerick.

Phyllis Fleming, Cork.

Kathleen McAuliffee, Kerry.

Nollaig Butler, Limerick.

John Skeates, Cork.

Mary Corcoron, Wicklow.

Maura Cullen, Dublin.

Josie Coffman, Wicklow.

Richard Brown, Kerry.

Alan Kitson, Meath.

D. Lloyd, Dublin.

Evelyn Browne, Kerry.

Tomas Dalton, Louth.

Margaret Darly, Louth.

Theresa Smyth, Offaly.

Catherine O'Donoghue, Kildare.

Maureen Heuston, Dublin.

Richard Craig.

P. Reilly, Dublin.

M. Ni Shuíleobhan, Tipperary.

Joe Hayes, Wicklow.

Mark Lucas, Cork.

Deirdre Bourke, Cork.

Nora Healy, Cork.

Mairin Kent, Waterford.

John Hogan, Kilkenny.

Rosemary Motherway, Cork.

Brigid Walsh, Tipperary.

John O'Mahony, Cork.

Ann Ryan, Tipperary.

B. Breen, Wicklow.

Niamh McCann, Dublin.

Deborah O'Connor, Kerry.

Brian O'Browne, Kerry.

Veronica Cramer, Cork.

E. Furlong, Dublin.

Stephen Loughman, Dublin.

Mary Clifton, Dublin.

Mary Cummins, Wexford.

Rosa Glacken, Meath.

Michael Quinn, Dublin.

Thomas P. Joyce, Mayo.

John Heffernan, Mayo.

Orlaith Benn, Dublin.

Hugh Sheridan, Dublin.

Sr. Kathleen O'Brien, South Pres. Cork.

Catherine Morgan, Clare.

Mary Gralton, Dublin.

Diarmuid Breathnach, Wicklow.

Catherine Gleeson, Tipperary.

Ingh Ní Dubhlain, Sligo.

Mary O'Shea, Roscommon.

Sean O'Ruain, Clare.

Seosamh O'Maolalai, Dublin.

Sheila Coyle, Cavan.

Guss O'Connell, Dublin M.C.C.

Maureen Cleary, Cork.

Dermot Mooney, Dublin.

Garrett Keegan, Cork.

S. McDonald, Tipperary.

Shraddna Burke Prehu, Galway.

Marion Kinsella, Dublin.

Bernadette McElligott, Kerry.

Dr. Padraig, O'Donnabhain, Kerry.

D. McGinley, Donegal.

Eileen O'Connell, Kerry.

Sheila Ryan, Waterford.

Ann Donohoe, Tipperary.

Pat Enright, Tipperary.

Mary O'Connell, Dublin.

CH Murray, Dublin.

Noirin Allen, Offaly.

Paul Ince, Dublin.

Patrick Fagan, Dublin.

Liam Tynan, Louth.

Philomena Davey.

Patrick O'Neill, Monaghan.

Brigid Hunt, Dublin.

Christopher Byrne, Dublin.

Brendan Greally, Mayo.

Chris Jennings, Dublin.

Pat McGonagle, Westmeath.

Tom McCarthy, Cork.

Cora Ní Ghamhna, Wicklow.

Gerry Kelleher, Cork.

David Shulman, Dublin.

Teresa Scully, Dublin.

Margaret Ryan, Tipperary.

Mike McInerney, Kildare.

Dom MacDonald, Monaghan.

Padraig O'Duibhir, Dublin.

Antony Foutz, Tipperary.

Maeve McCluskey @tinet

Joe O'Reilly. @indigo.ie

Eileen & Michael Longman Cork.

Marie Grant, Bedford, England.

Patricia Kerr, Dublin.

Angela Burt, Mayo.

Seamus Flanagan, Limerick.

Eleanor M. Ticher, Dublin.

Gerard J. Ahern. Galway.

Eileen Keane, Dublin.

M. McIvor, Dublin.

Ann Power, Wexford.

Maisie Caswell, Wicklow.

Tom O'Keefe, Kildare.

Richard Conway, Wexford.

Maureen Barry, Cork.

David Egan, Westmeath.

Alicia St Leger, Cork.

James Powell, Tipperary.

James Maher, Westmeath.

Martin Timoney, Sligo.

Kathleen Walsh, Kilkenny.

Helen Rinde, Cork.

Gerard Ryan, Dublin.

Bernard Coleman,Tipperary.

Teresa Carrig, Limerick.

Diarmuid O'Grada, Dublin.

Eileen O'Regan, Cork.

Derek Byrne, Dublin.

Ciaran Higgins, Donegal.

Anthony Keogh, Dublin.

Audrey Willits, Dublin

Sairseal O' Marcaigh,Dublin.

K.S. McGregor, Dublin.

Frances Shearer, Wicklow.

Tim O'Sullivan, Kerry.

Eileen O'Connor, Kerry.

Brian Martin, Dublin.

Nellie Prout, Waterford.

Maureen & Ian Kennedy, Louth.

Michael Sheridan, Dublin.

Harry Murphy, Dublin.

Paul Waldron, Tipperary.

Declan Crotty, Cork.

Malcolm Kelly, Cork.

Martin O'Leary, Cork.

David Sowby, Dublin.

Mary O'Gorman, Kilkenny.

Rose Mooney, Dublin.

Donal Collier, Dublin.

Mary O'Reilly, Westmeath.

Geraldine Coleman, Waterford.

Ann Young, Roscommon.

Aidan Power, Cork.

Angela Somerfield, Dublin.

Jim Fitzpatrick, Cork

Ciara Cantillon, Limerick

Denise Harte, Louth.

Walter Burghoff, Kerry.

Donal O'Sullivan, Cork.

Ann Doyle, Wexford.

Kay Lyons, Kerry.

Philomena McCloskey, Donegal.

Pat Stagg, Tipperary.

Mary Bowe, Waterford.

J. Desmond Hill, Cork.

Andrew Marsh, Kerry.

Mary English, Cork.

Alyn E. Fenn, Cork.

Veronica White, Kerry.

Margaret Teegan.

Margaret Sheehy, Cork.

Noreen and Gerry Murphy, Cork.

F.J. Steele, Cork.

Richard Cave, Donegal.

Sean O'Luing, Dublin.

Brid O'Brien, Tipperary.

Dr. M.A. Tierney, Kildare.

Harry McCauley, Westmeath.

Sorca Flemming, Tipperary.

Joseph Clancy, Dublin.

Sr. Mary Flanagan, Tipperary.

Proinsias Piogóid, Dublin.

Mairead ní Drisceol, Dublin.

Clara ni Annracháin, Cork.

Maolsheachlainn O Caollai, Dublin.

John McCarthy, Cork.

Liam Clare, Dublin

Caroline Farrell, Dublin

Eimear Greaney, Galway.

Mary Brown,.

Kay O'Keeffe, Douglas, Cork.

Chris Bailey, <cbailey@tcd.ie

Theresa McDonald, Offaly

Imogen Bertin, imogen@ctc.ie

William Keeling, keel@iol.ie

Donal D'Arcy, Cork.

Thomas Martin.

Mairead Mullaney

Josie O, Dublin .

Maire Mac Conghail, Dublin .

Siobhan Ryan, Dublin
John Steele, Librarian, Michael Smurfit Graduate
School of Business, U.C.D.
Isabelle Cartwright, Maynooth, Co. Kildare.
3 anonymous submissions.
82 individual submissions from Lucan
residents
60 submissions in response to 'Echo Island'
competition.

Organisations who made submissions

Cavan Adult Literacy Scheme.
Group submission from 273 Lucan school-goers.
Royal Irish Academy, Dublin.
O'Brien Press Ltd.
Irish Wheelchair Association, Galway.
Ballymun Youthreach, Dublin.
Irish Refugee Council.
County Kildare Archaeological Society.
Irish Association of Older People.
Sligo Family Centre
Bord na Gaeilge, Dublin.
Construction Industry Federation.
National Council for the Blind of Ireland.
Combat Poverty Agency.
GAYHIV Strategies, Dublin.
Kerry County Library
Dublin Heritage Group.
European Anti-Poverty Network.
Information Society Commission.
Dublin Corporation.
Age & Opportunity, Dublin.
County Kildare Leader II.
International Education Services, Kildare.
Library Association of Ireland
National Rehabilitation Board.
West Cork Enterprise Board, Cork.
Royal Irish Academy of Music, Dublin.
Irish Council of People with Disabilities, Waterford.
National Archives, Dublin.
Kilcock Heritage Group, Kildare.
Equality Liaison Committee, Dublin Public Libraries
Action South Kildare.
Westmeath County Library.
Celbridge Branch Library, Co. Kildare.
MRBI Ltd.

Centre for Cooperative Studies, UCC.
European Computer Driving License Ireland Ltd.
Dublin VEC Administration Centre.
Institute of Personnel & Development, London,
England.
An Comhchoiste Reamhscolaiochta.
Branch Librarians' Group, Dun Laoghaire - Rathdown
Libraries.
Dun-Laoghaire/Rathdown Co. Library.
European Anti Poverty Network Ireland.
Kare Adult Local Service.
National Adult Literacy Agency.
Dublin Heritage Group.
Dublin Corporation.
Ameritech, Library Services.
Prison Library Service.
Department of Justice, Equality and Law Reform
Irish Learning Support Association.
Joint submission from Fingal & South Dublin County
Libraries.
Irish Writers Union.
FAS.
Feach, Dublin.
Lendac Data Systems, Dublin .
Wexford County Council.
Open University Students Association.
IBEC/CIF
KPMG
Ulverscroft Foundation, England.
St. Josephs College, Ballinasloe
The Organic Collective, Community College Limerick.
Scoil Chronain, Rath Cuil, B.A.C..
Scoil Aine, Clondalkin Dublin.
Cnoc Mhuire Junior School, Dublin
Crooked House Theatre Co., Kildare
Marsh's Library
Portlaoise Citizens Information Centre
St. Joseph's School, Tipperary
Skerries Historical Society.
Michael Collins Cumann, Fine Gael, Cork.
Donaghmede Community Development Association.
Irish Business Publications.
Children's Books Ireland.
St. Peter's Apostle Junior School..
St Mary's National School, Dublin.
Sligo School Project.
Heritage Awareness Group.
Cnoc Mhuire Senior School, Dublin.

Scoil Mhuire gan Smol, Cork.
Rathnew Development Association, Wicklow.
St Anne's Senior School, Dublin.
Navan Road Community Council, Dublin.
Broadstone Studios, Dublin.
Forbairt, Cork.
Letterkenny Vocational School.
South Tipperary Arts Centre.
Friends of Tipperary Library.
National Centre for Guidance in Education.
Cavan County Council.